Teaching Poetry Writing
to Adolescents

Holly G. Singleton

Teaching Poetry Writing to Adolescents

Joseph I. Tsujimoto
Punahou School, Honolulu, Hawaii

ERIC Clearinghouse on Reading and Communication Skills
National Council of Teachers of English
1111 Kenyon Road, Urbana, Illinois 61801

Staff Editor: Jane M. Curran

Book Design: Tom Kovacs for TGK Design, interior; Michael Getz, cover

NCTE Stock Number 52260

Published 1988 by the ERIC Clearinghouse on Reading and Communication Skills and the National Council of Teachers of English, 1111 Kenyon Road, Urbana, Illinois 61801. Printed in the United States of America.

Office of Educational Research and Improvement U.S. Department of Education This publication was prepared with funding from the Office of Educational Research and Improvement, U.S. Department of Education, under contract no. 400-86-0045. Contractors undertaking such projects under government sponsorship are encouraged to express freely their judgment in professional and technical matters. Prior to publication, the manuscript was submitted to the National Council of Teachers of English for critical review and determination of professional competence. This publication has met such standards. Points of view or opinions, however, do not necessarily represent the official view or opinions of either the National Council of Teachers of English or the Office of Educational Research and Improvement.

Library of Congress Cataloging-in-Publication Data

Tsujimoto, Joseph I., 1946–
  Teaching poetry writing to adolescents.

  Bibliography: p.
  1. Poetry — Study and teaching (Secondary)
2. School verse, American. I. Title.
PN1101.T77 1988   808.1'07'12   88-5116
ISBN 0-8141-5226-0

To Michael: *You were right. It's a noble profession.*

To the students of Punahou School, Iolani School, and Seabury
Hall, Hawaii: *Thank you for sharing your visions. You have
taught me much.*

Contents

Foreword

This book was developed during the time period when the ERIC Clearinghouse on Reading and Communication Skills (ERIC/RCS) was sponsored by the National Council of Teachers of English. The Educational Resources Information Center (ERIC) is a national information system developed by the U.S. Department of Education and sponsored by the Office of Educational Research and Improvement (OERI). ERIC provides ready access to descriptions of exemplary programs, research and development reports, and related information useful in developing effective educational programs.

Through its network of specialized centers or clearinghouses, each of which is responsible for a particular educational area, ERIC acquires, evaluates, abstracts, and indexes current significant information and lists this information in its reference publications.

The ERIC system has already made available — through the ERIC Document Reproduction Service — a considerable body of data, including all federally funded research reports since 1956. However, if the findings of educational research are to be used by teachers, much of the data must be translated into an essentially different context. Rather than resting at the point of making research reports readily accessible, OERI has directed the ERIC clearinghouses to commission authorities in various fields to write information analysis papers.

This book, then, is the most recent of dozens of practitioner-oriented texts developed by ERIC/RCS under the sponsorship of NCTE, 1972-1987. The Clearinghouse and the Council hope that the materials are helpful in clarifying important educational issues and in improving classroom practice.

Karl Koenke
Associate Director, 1975–87
ERIC/RCS

Introduction

When I read the first draft of this book, I was pleasantly stunned by Joseph Tsujimoto's insight, vigor, and dedication. Here is a classroom teacher speaking in his own voice, an authentic voice, making use of a formidable understanding of literature and teaching methods but declining to write a manuscript guarded by heavy references to all the right theorists and researchers. I found the manuscript persuasive because Tsujimoto is a well-read teacher who dares to invent in the classroom, to recast his teaching based on students' responses, and to share the results of his joyful struggles with fellow teachers.

Those who previewed successive drafts had reactions similar to mine. One wrote, "This is passionate writing. The student samples are beautiful. The grade levels they represent are the great void in public schools — the junior high school years, ... the years that students decide whether to believe in the value of learning or to turn it off. Tsujimoto has tapped and exemplified the value of models in teaching writing." Another said, "This is a fine manuscript by a master teacher. ... I feel that the student poetry is outstanding and uplifting. ... I was convinced that I was in the hands of someone who knows and loves poetry and someone who knows how to teach it." Others wrote more briefly: "It's a lovely book." "I am impressed and inspired. Print this!"

Many of Tsujimoto's poetry assignments call to mind the work of Kenneth Koch in *Wishes, Lies, and Dreams* and *Rose, Where Did You Get That Red?* But Tsujimoto, a full-time classroom teacher, goes beyond Koch's work. One reader noted that the Koch materials are almost formulaic compared to Tsujimoto's assignments, which "shape the attempts of the students without unduly constraining them, as some of Koch's exercises seem to do." But I don't want to pit one good teacher against another. What we have in the professional literature is a mainstream of helpful and creative ideas from writers like Kenneth Koch, Daniel Fader, and Ken Macrorie — and Joseph Tsujimoto writes in that tradition.

None of which is to say that this book is the ultimate inservice packet on teaching poetry to middle and secondary school students.

For one thing, many of the students Tsujimoto teaches are quite above average. No technique or assignment transfers automatically from one school setting to another, especially when school populations differ dramatically. Nevertheless, Tsujimoto's teaching concepts and procedures strike me as highly adaptable. The thoughtful teacher-reader will find a wealth of ideas to adapt and will no doubt generate great excitement about poetry by emulating Tsujimoto's approaches.

"Adapt" and "emulate" are apt terms here. Like a good teacher, Tsujimoto does not overprescribe. His text is lucid in presentation and rich in suggestion, assuming that the audience will bring to it a disposition to evaluate, expand, revise, and integrate according to individual teaching styles and varying school situations.

In a sense this book extends the range of publications in the ERIC/NCTE program. Our usual books — TRIP (Theory and Research Into Practice) booklets, essay collections, research summaries, and the like — are enriched by this absorbing teacher narrative laced with samples of outstanding student writing products. I hope we'll have occasion to see more texts in this exciting genre.

> Charles Suhor
> Deputy Executive Director
> NCTE

Preface

The purpose of this book is to serve as a general model for the teaching of poetry writing. Though originally intended for teachers of seventh and eighth graders, it is equally applicable for elementary, high school, and college teachers. The governing principle behind the book's collection and organization of ideas stems from Hemingway's *iceberg,* the bulk of which lies below the surface. That is, all that I know — all that I have learned, borrowed, and conceived myself — gives force to what little I teach. Chapters 1 and 2 (the "hidden" portion of the *iceberg*) contain the underlying assumptions that account for and lead to the success of the student poetry in chapter 3.

Chapter 1 introduces me and my students; compares junior high school students, in terms of aesthetic honesty, to elementary and high school students; and introduces Professor Konstantinos Lardas, one of my college teachers. The pivotal assumption in this chapter is that in a teacher-student setting, Maria Montessori's *real learning* and Carl Rogers's *real growth* often cannot proceed until students are inspired by the teacher; and that what the students ultimately learn is the teacher, assimilating — because of the teacher's passionate conviction — the reverence for writing and literature, the standards, and, sometimes, the ambitions of the teacher.

Chapter 2, "Models and Teaching Designs," establishes the theoretical groundwork upon which poetry assignments are designed, sequenced, presented, revised, evaluated, and completed, resulting in individual poetry books. The first assumption in this chapter is that if students are to be inspired, the teacher must indulge his or her feelings, not only in selecting examples that are truly admired or loved, but, more especially, in the personal way the teacher reads those examples to the students. The second assumption is that inspiration is best achieved when the teacher uses student works as primary examples, when the teacher continually requires originality, and when the teacher, to guide individuals, exercises his or her expertise in criticizing and evaluating student works — a difficult task where poetry is concerned, since many teachers, for various sensitive reasons, withhold their criticisms.

Chapter 3, "Poems and Poetry Assignments," is the manifest portion of the iceberg. It presents specific poetry assignments that have worked for me; it offers suggestions on how the assignments might be presented; and it reproduces examples of student poetry that can be used to explain and illustrate the assignments. The student poems, *in toto*, reveal to my students their *own* literary tradition — the tradition established by previous students of their own age and grade level in their own school and a tradition of which they and their work will become a part. This tradition is invaluable to my students and me, since the best of the tradition is the standard against which they and I can measure and fairly evaluate new student work.

I teach poetry because it gives students a way of crystallizing and publicly expressing private emotions that otherwise might be impossible to communicate. On the other hand, I also teach poetry because it persuades students to hear and recognize the private feelings of others. As Hart Crane suggests (in the epigraph to chapter 3), poetry extends our experience and broadens our consciousness, making us aware of other people's points of view, other people's visions of history, the cosmos, and God. In this one sense alone lies its most practical function: to humanize and elevate our race as a civilized species, cultivating sensitive, open-minded human beings — which is the true vocation for which we are preparing our students. This is why our students practice the arts.

I wish to thank Patricia Creel, Richelle Fujioka, Marilyn Stassen-McLaughlin, Lani Uyeno, and Duane Yee for helping me resee, recast, and reorganize my thinking. I wish especially to thank my wife, Sharon Tsujimoto, for her tolerance and advice as she proofread through each stage of the development of the book.

Joseph I. Tsujimoto

1 Students and Teachers

When I first heard that this quarter we were going to do a poetry book, I nearly died. At that time, I had very little experience in reading, let alone writing, poetry. To me, poetry was a bunch of complex rhyming words, in a funny arrangement, that has some obscure meaning, written by a freelance weirdo. Of course, with this idea in mind, I was ready for a big surprise.

— David Bell (grade 8)

It's a great feeling to know that there is a way to express my emotions without any fear of persecution and to even get praise for it.

— Edward Henigin (grade 8)

The feeling received when finishing a poem *that you know* is good is one of exhilaration. You have created something great; for that short while, you are a genius.

— Stepen Di Mauro (grade 8)

I used to think that the best thing one could do with junior high school students was to send them off to a desert island for two years, hoping (unrealistically) that they wouldn't annihilate each other. I knew that if I had *me* as one of my own students I would have booted me out of class.

But I couldn't help it. My body was going crazy. Even my mind was glandular. And nothing ever fit my face — not my hands, my feet, or my voice. Few things ever felt right, ever felt the way they were supposed to feel. For I was the ideal idealist, mercilessly aware of my shortcomings. So I ate. Got fat (Gosh, who is that kid?) and held hands with an anorexic during fire drills. I had a knack for algebra and became the first Japanese Freddie Eynesford Hill in an all-black production of *My Fair Lady* at Junior High School 43, Harlem, since I was the first seventh grader with a nice tenor voice.

Besides, I was in love with a Puerto Rican flower named Luz — a wonderful, if bittersweet, two-year obsession. I followed her everywhere, and at the change of every class I waited opposite her room to watch her, with groveling eyes, enter and exit the door. She was constantly on my mind, worrying me, invading my daydreams; and only in my daydreams did we ever meet and, impossibly, talk!

Then, too, there was Blumenthal and Hector Maldonado, Oyama, Marco, and Provenzano, Ruggiere and Muller-Thyme (John and Tom), Calnan, Pops, and Jimmy Sullivan, especially Jimmy Sullivan (to whom I owe my knowledge of nine ball and three-cushion billiards, which led, later, to the vice principal's inviting me to leave, immediately and forever, George Washington High School). To play was the thing, whether the street lights lit one by one down Amsterdam Avenue, across 125th Street, all the way up to City College, or snowflakes fell on the basketball court at P.S. 125, my alma mater.

The stifling heat of home and sedentary parents felt oppressive. I was ecstatic and melancholy, irritable and sarcastic; nor did anyone do anything as it should be done. For life should be fulfilled perfectly right now. Patience was for old men. True, home was where the heart was, so long as the heart could be vented. To argue with my mother or to pester my brother or sisters was at least *something*, if not drama. But I needed to do something more.

More than twenty years later, I relived my hopes, sentiments, and anxieties through my students' eyes, and realized what I have been doing with them is right.

And what have I done? Nothing very much. Nor anything very new. As artists do to themselves, I merely encouraged them to transform their "handicaps" — their feelings of being odd — into virtues. Of course, I didn't mention handicaps or feelings of being odd. Instead, I talked about originality. I said that in writing or painting or dance, originality is the one thing that distinguishes a work from another and determines its worth; that originality is the one thing that sets them off as the individual human beings that they are. As I think back, nothing appealed to me more than the teacher challenging my creativity. Boy, I was going to do something that no one had ever done and make buildings tremble. That kind of confidence is assumed by youth when their imaginations are fired. Nothing is beyond their reach. Few truly important things really are.

Students

Despite the claim of child psychologists — that students during puberty reach an intellectual plateau — I believe that puberty is one of the most fertile periods of a youth's life. Consider alone the enormous energy adolescents possess. And I mean this in a positive sense, since this energy is vital, seeking only the discipline of those who will guide with understanding.

Puberty, of course, is not as fertile a period as the first-grade years that Kenneth Koch and Donald Graves write about. We see in first graders an aesthetic honesty we will rarely see again until writers learn to emulate, in their full maturity, their original innocence. However, comparatively speaking, first graders have not yet had the dubious good fortune of being "educated" in the conventional beliefs embraced by their peers or promoted through mass media. Mature writers have learned to hold these beliefs suspect, or adopt them under strict conditions. Junior high school students do not have the purity of faith of either group. On the other hand, they are not as inured to conventional beliefs as most high school students and adults.

For one thing, most high school students (when they do write poetry seriously) are self-conscious to a fault, writing poems that sound and feel "dissonant." The reader can sense in their writing a divided attention, not totally concentrated on the subject at hand. Instead, enamored of the language, impressed by the adult poets they have read, influenced by fashionable or effete ideas (a necessary phase through which young minds must struggle), they strain after effect, undermining the purity of their vision.

For Rilke, this purity of vision, this totality of attention — this aesthetic honesty — is nothing less than love; and nothing less than love can encourage out of words, colors, sounds, and things the mysterious life they possess. But, as Rilke (1965, 48–49) says,

> . . . if the thing sees that you are preoccupied, with even a mere particle of your interest, it shuts itself up again . . . it refuses to give you its heart, to disclose to you its patient being, its sweet sidereal constancy that makes it so like the constellations! If a thing is to speak to you, you must regard it for a certain time *as the only one that exists*, as the one and only phenomenon, which, thanks to your laborious and exclusive love, is now placed at the center of the Universe, and there, in that incomparable place, is this day attended by the Angels.

For junior high school students, and elementary students especially, such self-forgetfulness seems almost a natural state of mind when they are attending to things. This state of mind is what my former students are trying to grasp again, as they recently tried to explain to English teachers at a curriculum-day workshop. They wished they had *now* the confidence and seemingly effortless fluency that they had when they were younger and less knowing. For high school students and adults, reaching back and experiencing that state of mind is supreme achievement, while for younger people (though what they produce may seem naive or simplistic), the experience is commonplace.

For example, one of the most difficult things in the world to do is talk about oneself. The following are excerpts from individual Self Portrait poems (treated more fully in chapter 3, assignment number 16).

The boy walks back from P.E.;
girl opening her locker says, "Hi,"
he says, "Hi," but he thinks, thank
you

— Howard Lao (grade 8)

What's happening to Me? he asks. No
kiss for mom any more

— Mike Wilson (grade 8)

Thin white legs
Protruding from a
Sadly underdeveloped
Torso.
An American Ethiopian

— Edward Henigin (grade 8)

His mother:
He hides
So I can't talk to him
About his dirty room
        the dirty kitchen
        the dog's mistakes
        the leaf-filled patio
Oh, there he is —
SAMMY!

— Sam Onaga (grade 8)

Although I like war,
I dislike nuclear weapons
I think we should go back to clubs
        and knives
It would be more fun

— Gavin Lohmeier (grade 8)

Dear Lord,
   Help me
with everything.
If not that
Have me   be
good

— Alton Clingan (grade 8)

Will you kids
Shut up   Slam!
Ya   Slam!
Shut up already
I'm still trying
to sleep   Slam!
This family!
Slam!

— Julie Kometani (grade 7)

To my little cousins
I am a giant
from a place so small.
It is a bump in the Pacific Ocean.
I read them stories
and brush the little girl's hair
and disappear
beyond the window.
Now a name
mentioned at breakfast

— Paula Goodman (grade 8)

My
mind is always thinking
      like a swimming
fish

— Keith Krasniewski (grade 7)

Teachers

Maria Montessori says that *anything that is truly learned* is self-taught. This theory implies its complement: Carl Rogers says that *the only learning which significantly influences behavior* is self-discovered, self-appropriated learning. But the teacher can facilitate this learning growth by providing students with choices, options. Both theories are founded on teacher self-effacement and a confidence in the students' drive to continually re-create themselves.

My argument with Montessori and Rogers is that both — through their selfless concern for their students — neglect themselves as pivotal figures in their own classrooms. It is their passionate presence, their voice, their words that inspire others in wanting to learn. And without inspiration, no true learning, no true growth — no self-empower-ment — can proceed. In a teacher-student setting, as both Montessori and Rogers exemplify, what is ultimately learned is the teacher!

What I learned at City College of New York was Gus — Professor Konstantinos Lardas.

Duende

> Whoever inhabits that bull's hide stretched between the Jucar, the Guadalete, the Sil, or the Pisuerga — no need to mention those lion-colored waves churned up the Plata — has heard it said with a certain frequency: "Now that has real *duende!*"
>
> — Federico García Lorca (1955, 154)

As a freshman at C.C.N.Y. interested in architecture, I took an upper-level English course called the Techniques of Verse in order to fulfill G.I. Bill credit requirements. As a stranger, I knew no one in class, least of all our professor, the Greek poet Konstantinos Lardas.

At the bell, he leaned into the classroom, shoulders and head only, and smiled at us oddly. Leaning back, tilting his head, and raising his dark eyebrows, he looked up at the room number stenciled above the door. Then stepping over the threshold, in dark blue slacks, he looked at us again with that odd smile lighting up his amber face.

Who was this man? He seemed senile, though he wasn't really old. Maybe he drank; there was a rubberiness about his jowls. He stepped gingerly toward us, like an old man, and greeted us almost as though we were children. I don't recall very much of this first class, except that he seemed to stammer like a child groping for words, appealing (with one hand on his forehead) to nearby students (while motioning them toward him with the other) to give him the words that had slipped his mind. "Oh, you know what I mean" (his hand shaking). "Yes, yes, that's the one."

Then suddenly it didn't matter any more whether his gestures, his fumbling after words, his being "old" were all a ploy. For he was ingratiating, as warm as his soft dark clothes and the books he read, horn-rimmed glasses at the end of his nose. And how he read! I could hear each word, sharp, edged with the roughness of his voice, charged with large and lofty feelings. I can see him now, his shoulders and head imperceptibly nodding as he emphasized the words; for what passion he had for words, as though he could not contain them within himself, as when he told us of the first time he had read Hopkins. Then how he thrilled us with his stammerings and his hands and his shoulders, communicating his awe.

In the first few weeks he read us fragments of Sappho, Sacco's farewell letter before his execution, the catalog of whale names at the beginning of *Moby Dick*, Hopkins, and Lorca's essay "The Duende: Theory and Divertissment." Soon, we loved words as much as he did, especially Lorca's "Duende" (1955, 154):

> Black sounds: so said the celebrated Spaniard, thereby concurring
> with Goethe, who, in effect, defined the *duende* when he said,
> speaking of Paganini: "A mysterious power that all may feel and
> no philosophy explain."

For me, Konstantinos Lardas — the embodiment of passionate conviction (which leads to the duende) — is the model against which I measure my teaching; the model against which I measure literature. Lardas is what I learned.

2 Models and Teaching Designs

The Potter

The poet is like a potter
shaping and molding words onto
paper
He spins the wheel,
pressing detail and action
into crevices of phrases
and baking feeling into every line.

— Tracie Tsukano (grade 8)

Nothing deadens a work quicker than weak feelings. Strong feelings, on the other hand, enhance a work, even if we were to read it in a foreign tongue. For example, my friend Larry Traynor, who used to moonlight singing at weddings and funerals, played for me a recording of his reading of Wallace Stevens's "River of Rivers in Connecticut." Although I didn't understand the poem at the time (it was intellectually foreign to me), I was nonetheless moved by the rhythm of the lines, the sounds of the words, the powerful feelings in Larry's voice, and I came to love the work almost as much as Larry did. So it happens with our students. Because we are moved, they will be moved — they who are experts in reading us.

Choosing Examples

Much depends, then, on what we choose to read as examples. I use the following three student poems, as well as others, to teach extended metaphor (described more fully in chapter 3, assignment number 9) and to introduce the tradition of writing poems about poems, poetry, and the poet.

Vulture in a Poet

The poet sits and waits for an idea
like a vulture in a dead tree
waiting for a fair chance

His gripped hands nervously tapping the desk
    like a vulture pacing the sky

At last an idea strikes as he grasps
    his paper
like a vulture diving for his feast
    his mouth opened wide

          — Brandy Spoehr (grade 7)

    The Poem in the River

As a river flows
so flows a poem

into every
crack and crevice

rearranging soil
inventing a new geography

it changes the
face of the Earth

          — Kale Braden (grade 8)

        hands

He creates
with a mind from above
taking others beyond
the present world
with his brush
and his pen

The rainbow falls from his hands
splashing unending color
shattering reality —
a rock thrown through a picture window

in his mind
in his painting
in his hands
      The sun explodes

          — unknown student (grade 10)

In presenting this assignment — in presenting every assignment, in fact — I read numerous student examples: many that demonstrate the rules for extended metaphor and many, like "hands," that break or change the rules in wonderful ways.

Student poems often make the best examples; their impact is large. Mention to the class a poet's grade level and name, and you will spark immediate interest, rousing curiosity, attuning (it seems evident now) the listeners' critical ears. Not only do the students share with the poet similar experiences and sensibilities, but more importantly, the young poet shows other students the potential quality of work that *they* themselves can produce. On the other hand, if students know that a work is authored by an adult (because they have been told or because it is evident through sophistication of the language or ideas), the work will appear beyond the students' reach. Often, what makes the adult work inaccessible is not so much its language or ideas (which we can lead them to understand), as it is the impossibility of their "duplicating" such work. Skills aside, they have little interest in wanting to. (This is not to say I don't use any adult examples at all. I do. The point is, they are not my primary examples.)

Finally, as we accumulate more and more examples of the students' best work, we help them establish for themselves their own literary tradition, to be used in helping them teach themselves and to become a standard for evaluating new student work.

Options and Limitations

Paradoxically, giving students *many* examples, by both students and adults, can encourage the writing of original poetry. Originality can best be realized through freedom of choice, which becomes meaningful only when one is aware of many options. So I give students as many examples as I can, not just to fire their imaginations with good works, but to increase their awareness of options as well.

First, the sheer number of examples makes students feel like emotional kaleidoscopes. Second, the redundancy illustrates the rules for extended metaphor and, especially, the exceptions to the rules — creating more options.

In the end, freedom of choice really means freedom to select one's limitations. That is, in the act of choosing for oneself, one simultaneously imposes limitations upon oneself. Though, at first, the teacher imposes the larger limitation ("Write an Extended Metaphor poem on poetry, poems, or the poet"), the student later imposes the specific ones. Allison Higa (grade 8) said, "I think I'll describe the poet as a circus clown, remembering what he looks like and how he acts," and wrote the following:

Clown

Clowns are supposed to be happy.
They're always funny, so they must be happy,
at least most of the time.
A poet's words are like a clown's makeup.
A wide mouth painted to smile, a stark white
face, stars for eyes.
His clothing is hilarious: gigantic, floppy saddle
shoes, bum suits or polka dots. A fake burning
building, a net without a center, a midget car.
These are the things he's based his act on.
Some sad, mostly humorous.
He leaves a feeling behind, a feeling you can
remember for a long time.

Gina Pagliaro (grade 8) stated, "I think I'll make a poem describing poetry as technology, using three similes — a technician, an operator, and a machine — rolled into one," before she wrote this poem:

Technical Similarities

The poet is like a technician
Mending and repairing
Words that are used
Omitting the trite.

The poet is attached to his work
As the telephone operator is
     often entangled.

The poem is like a machine
Walking, talking, showing action.

Do you know what I mean?

As Ann E. Berthoff (1981) says, it is precisely the choosing of limits — amalgamating, differentiating, classifying, comparing, discarding, and so forth — that constitutes the composing process. And as Rollo May (1975) comments, it is the struggle with limits that is actually the source of creative production. Sam Onaga (grade 8) struggles directly with the limits of his own experience as a writer who wants to make fine things, conscious of what works against him as well as for him.

The Writer

He sits
In front of a typewriter

Typing about:
Plot
Flow
Conflict
Character
Drama
Style
Effect
Doing his job.

Other times he is writing about
John Doe
His dark past
His great future
His tears
His smiles
His good and evil
About John's inside.

It is John's inside
That so moves us,
That dazzles
And shines.
And takes out of the dark
A part of his maker
A part of *his* story.

More important than students' knowing extended metaphor is their grasping, more strongly with each assignment, the pivotal notion of originality. For one thing, they know that originality ultimately precludes their imitating the poetry already created. Now they must discover for themselves that it *can be*. In a sense, we confine the students in a prison whose walls they must shatter. In this way they emancipate their own minds, realizing further the enormous creative power within their hands.

Derivations

Every original work, in one way or another, is derived from other works. T. S. Eliot (1950) makes this clear in his essay "Tradition and the Individual Talent." The writer speaks not only with the voice of his own age but also with the voices of his eminent predecessors. Eliot's "April is the cruellest month" recalls Chaucer's "Whan that Aprill with his shoures soote," which also "begot" the springtimes of Nashe, Herrick, and Hopkins; and as the structuralists point out, Chaucer's spring also begot the winter in Hardy's "The Darkling Thrush," as well as the fall in Keats's "To Autumn." A seminal work implies not only its opposite but also every other possible variant to which the seminal work can be transformed. Thereafter, each derivative work itself can become a seminal work, spawning its own variations. In this way, Eliot says, the past directs the present, while the present, the truly original derivation, alters, ever so slightly, the entire tradition, which at any moment in time is complete.

Traditions abound, from rock music to stamps to textbooks. This book, for example, is derived in part from Kenneth Koch's *Wishes, Lies, and Dreams* (1980) and *Rose, Where Did You Get That Red?* (1974). In both, Koch demonstrates the dramatic effectiveness of modeling as a tool in teaching elementary school children to write poetry. As a derivative work, this book differs from Koch's in its assumptions, offering theoretical underpinnings — alternative opinions and strategies — geared to the teaching of adolescents.

Now let me make a promise beforehand.

Most teachers, as you know, are always on the lookout for new ideas in order to improve their teaching. In so doing, they collect ideas found in publications (which often report the ideas found in other publications); they borrow ideas from other teachers (who in turn have borrowed ideas from still others); and, of course, they invent and share their own ideas — equally without thought to attribution.

This is especially true when teachers hunt for, find, or invent writing assignments. I think many teachers instinctively view assignments as anonymous ballads that have been passed from town to town, passed down through generations by word of mouth, modified over and again by the many voices that sing them. Like ballads, assignments are sources that belong to the community, practiced and perpetuated by its experts for the benefit of its people. The teachers' concern is: Does it work for me? Will it work now? If not now, when? How? All that I can promise is that I will note derivative sources where I can.

All the poems in this book are also derivations. Of these, there are three kinds. First is the derivation "born" of a specific poem. For example, the Self Portrait poem (or definition poem) springs from Wallace Stevens's "Thirteen Ways of Looking at a Blackbird." However, instead of an animal as its subject (as in Stevens's work) or instead of an object as its subject (as Koch directs his children to choose), the students are asked to turn Stevens's strategy on themselves. Like Stevens's blackbird, the presence of the self is manifest in each stanza, which can be "seen" as a unique sketch on a transparency. Like Stevens's blackbird, the self is defined by the total number of stanzas, which can be "seen" as the total number of transparencies laid one atop another, resulting in a complex symbol. Red-haired Eric Meyer (grade 7) shows us how he sees himself.

Self Portrait

A dark snowy day.
The pine trees whisper
As he looks up at them.
He catches a word about loneliness,
He tramples back to his house.

He peers at an ant
Crawling on a flower
He tries to decipher
The pattern of its dance.

He whistles as he walks.
The wind
Rises around
Him
Telling him
To be quiet.
It wonders
How he could dare
Interrupt
The song
The crickets play
At this hour.

The birds fly past him
Looking at him
Up in the magnolia tree
And wonder if he's one
Of their kind.

He runs into his room
To play with his kitten
He leaves as soon as he comes,
He looks back

And sees it licking itself
With a confused face.

Snow
Covered, as far as can be seen.
There are two things moving
A red bird
A small figure
Kicking the snow.

He is such a brainy
Pest, he hears his sister
Say to his mom.

He sees himself
Through the gates of clocks
A careful one
Stepping through time stones
Cautiously.

As he studies
He is of five minds
Combined in one.

He stays still
As he holds up
A can of seed
A bird comes
And feeds
From his hands
As if he were a statue.

In a telescope
He sees stars being born
And dying . . .
He wonders if it is
The stars' way
of telling him
What his life
Will be.

Second is the derivation "born" of a traditional type of poetry (e.g., poems that embody a traditional form or that address traditional topics or themes). For example, Chris Peters (grade 7) talks about love, using the sonnet form.

Love, a Feeling

Love is a feeling between a mixed pair
Upon first sight or after a long, long time
It creates a spirit, a world to share
Like a silent person, speaking in mime
Love, like wine, must age to taste just right
The vines of both bear fruit of varied hue.
While wine makes its choice, either red or white
Love cannot be limited to so few.
Love, like an orchestra, brings together
People of many different sections
It ties all voices one to another
Through the emotion of shared affection
Let love of two or more be justly earned
And not diminished by other things yearned.

Third is the derivation "born" of the unique literary traditions that
the individual has consciously or unconsciously assimilated. For example, the following surrealistic poem (by an unknown eighth grader)
was no doubt founded on his or her understanding of fairy tales,
fantasies, science fiction, comics, the drug culture, cartoons, music,
and movies.

Penguin

The skunk opened the door to the sewing
machine and got out.
He was pink.
He flew to the attendant, took the gas hose
and emptied his tank with ethyl lipstick.
He spilled it on his shabby purple socks,
which got dizzy and spaced out.
He looked down just as they burst into flames.
Immediately he took out his radio to block himself
from the smoke, so that he wouldn't turn into an
Infection.
Desperate for air, he took a sniff of fumes.
He got sick on an orange Arab standing
Next to him.
It had the license plate GLUE.
The ethyl stopped flowing so he pumped it back
into the attendant.

Out of his pocket aquarium, he took his
Fur credit cards. He gave them to the Blue-Gray
Shirt,
Who burned and then snorted them.
He wheeled around and said "Crazy Tuna."
The skunk then inked the shirt's face,
Jumped on his sewing machine,
And trucked back to the Sears Indian Reservation.

In general, there are only two kinds of writing: derivations, which draw on traditions, and imitations, which are bland copies. Sadly, most of the time our students submit the latter to us in bulk.

Making Assignments

In another approach aimed at getting students to write, three simple characteristics of all poems are identified.

1. They have a subject.
2. They have some kind of emotional impact.
3. They are constructed of verbal strategies to which we can give meanings.

If we turn the above statements into questions, they act as a rubric that can help us generate any number of possible writing assignments.

1. What, to you, is the poem about?
2. What is the poem's impact on you?
3. What strategies in the poem allow you to give meanings to it?

Simply take any poem that you truly admire, and identify one or two of its outstanding characteristics according to the rubric. I never apply more than two questions to the poem when making an assignment. Often I apply only one.

For example, I have always admired Whitman's "The Compost." Among other things, I like the idea that life is born of dead things. In answering the first question — what is the poem about? — I discovered this was my "seminal" poem for a category called Paradox Poems (or poems about apparent contradictions — see chapter 3, assignment number 12). Then I hunted up Robinson Jeffers's "The Great Explosion" (where, oddly, the root of all things is "faceless violence"); Blake's "The Tiger" (why did God, who made the lamb, also make the ferocious tiger?); and my friend Paul Wood's unpublished poem "Attraction" (where "Love is a great garlic sandwich"). Here was the beginning of my repertoire. Soon after, these poems became secondary examples, read after the poems written by students. The following example was written by Keli Sato (grade 7).

Behind Her Eyes

Though girls do say that they
hate boys,
we know that isn't so.
For every time the boy goes by
we see their red cheeks glow.

Still yet the boys confront her,
and look her in the eyes,
and ask her, "You do like him,"
and she says, "No." and lies.

But yet when girls confront her
she shares her secrets dear,
and at a slumber party
they're spread for all to hear.

She told them to keep a secret
this was her happy dream,
but telling them *this* secret
insures they'll spill the beans.

The news shot out like wildfire
as fast as beans will grow
but she actually wanted this to happen,
she wanted him to know.

So what's the whole big secret?
Why did she wait days?
Why not get it over with —
a woman has her ways.

Often we work the other way around when making assignments. Starting off with a literary concept that we would like our students to know, we then hunt about for examples. Making assignments this way is often more difficult than making assignments from poems we already love. Sometimes we can't find the examples that fulfill our purpose, especially if what we want them to know is a verbal strategy. We are always looking for the ideal example that will do its job with ruthless speed, where a point of literary understanding is the preeminent point the poem must demonstrate. So we find ourselves talking about parts of poems or secondary issues. Let me explain.

I wanted my students to understand that poems often operate according to various sorts of logic other than chronology or linearity, when moving from one set of words to another. In hunting for examples, I encountered two seemingly insurmountable problems. First, poets move between words in innumerable ways; second, the most striking aspects of the poems I found were the subjects and the emotional impact, not the poets' way of advancing their ideas. These problems, though, would foil my intentions, deflecting my students' attention from what I wanted them to know, or would suggest to them that my first concern was not the poem itself. The only solution to these particular problems was to invent my own poem "Snow Tracks" (the Circle Poem assignment), from which students derived their own poems, as shown in chapter 3, assignment number 3.

My point is *not* that we write our own poetry examples for the verbal strategies we want to teach. I am saying instead that it is easier making assignments with poems we already know and enjoy, many having dominant verbal strategies that we can lead students to appreciate.

Organizing Assignments

The three characteristics common to all poems suggest categories under which we can organize poetry assignments. I organized the following assignments under the characteristic that seemed to dominate the students' attention.

1. *Subject*
   Change Poem
   List of Twelve
   Animal Poem
   Visual Response Poem
   Form Poem
   Self Portrait
   Invitation Poem

2. *Emotional Impact*
   Memory Poem
   Bitterness Poem

Paradox Poem
Awe Poem
Teacher Poem
End Poem

3. *Verbal Strategies*
Found Poem
Two-Word Poem
Circle Poem
Transformation Poem
Extended Metaphor

Organizing assignments in this manner can help in planning a unit, a quarter, or a semester of teaching. Depending on the time we have and what our students already know, we can choose and order our assignments easily for our own ends. My goal is to teach the students as much as I can within a quarter, so that they have at least twenty poems to make into poetry books. My students do little more than listen to poetry, write poetry, and read poetry to the class. (Actually, they write a total of twenty-six poems. I have excluded from this text nine of the more conventional assignments, like the haiku, sonnets, and poems written in response to music.)

Another approach to organizing poetry assignments (that found in chapter 3 of this text) suggests incremental teaching: the Found Poem can come first because it focuses on lining, spacing, and other fundamental conventions; the Two-Word Poem follows, focusing on similitude; next come the Circle Poem, based on associative progression, the Change Poem, employing chronological leaping, and the Transformation Poem, using diction as a means of expressing the transmutation of one thing into another. That is, one could rationalize various logical progressions for the assignments — as I do, and intend, for the teaching of craft. Yet, I know, too, that learning an art, as opposed to a craft, transcends block-by-block learning.

To be honest, I am not sure that my students fully see the connections among the techniques that they initially practice. What I do know, however, is that they are wonderfully befuddled, disoriented, puzzled, and bemused by the singularity of the assignments and the peculiarity of their teacher. They know from the outset that they are embarking on something new — a trip whose each step can never be anticipated, like the trip we ideally take when experiencing the finest poems.

As when students read a fine poem, and we gain satisfaction in their discovering an original meaning for a single part — we are satisfied with the understanding that they do manifest when they are deeply engaged in writing their own poetry. More important, then, than ordering assignments like building blocks is maintaining that heightened sense of wonder, oddness, beauty, challenge, and excitement that will empower them to step over the edge.

Presenting Assignments

For many teachers the presentation of an assignment amounts to little more than announcing its directives. If they do not also provide guidance during revision, the writing assignment becomes a test, whether the test is overnight, over the weekend, or over the semester.

At the very minimum, as I pointed out earlier, we must expose the students to as many examples as possible, to make them aware of their options. There are times when reading examples alone is sufficient preparation, as with assignments that focus on feelings or on the subject of the poem. For Bitterness Poems, the examples, the angry reading I sometimes give the class, and the comments I make aloud to myself (about insensitivity, cruelty, and so forth) make the assignment clear. For other assignments, it is often necessary to provide additional preparation as well. These instances, obviously, are determined by the nature of the assignment. For Two-Word Poems, which focus on unusual similarities, students first play a word association game, exercising their associative skills.

Discussion is of great importance. This involves more than fielding questions about the assignment and forewarning students of the difficulties others have experienced before them. It should also involve leading them to discover the strategy you want them to exploit, and sharing ideas and opinions, anecdotes and stories, which are often the most interesting parts of the presentation.

The following illustrates the kind of thinking I exercised — the preparatory thought necessary for me — when preparing the presentation for the Awe Poem assignment. Let me say, right away, that the assignment did not succeed as well as I hoped, I think because I was overconfident about my stories and examples and so did not follow through with student brainstorming and freewriting (for homework) and in-class defining, which I initially intended them to do (see below).

First, I will give the students a copy of Keats's "On First Looking into Chapman's Homer" and lead them to what Keats had felt. Then I think I'll tell them my experience in seeing a scene from *Lawrence of Arabia* or *Amadeus* (maybe show them a tape?). Or maybe I will recount the first time I went to Yankee Stadium, when I saw Mickey Mantle hit a home run in the bottom of the ninth with a man on first. (He hit the ball on an ascending line, striking the fancy iron facade of the overhanging eaves of the top deck, which circled three-quarters of the ballpark — and I will tell them what I felt when the ball struck and the whole stadium rang like a gong with the vibrating iron. Bong!) On the subject of awesome power, I will then read W. S. Merwin's "Leviathan" and follow up with Ishmael's meditation on the mysterious head of the sperm whale. (I put that head before you. Read it if you can.) Or perhaps I should leap over that to Macbeth's "tomorrow" speech, first telling them the story in short (preparing them nicely for the play when we study it in the third quarter). Do I then dare read them the opening of *Paradise Lost*, ending with Milton's awesome promise: to "justify the ways of God to men"? I'm tempted. In any case, I'll have God appear out of the whirlwind, reading parts of Job, who not only heard God speak, but *saw!*

For homework, they will brainstorm all the instances in which they ever felt awe, freewriting a half-page on three of these experiences. The next day in class they will freewrite a definition for *awe*, which they can share with each other without my input.

Then I will tell them to write an Awe Poem (chapter 3, assignment number 13) based on one of their freewritings. After they revise their "final" drafts, I can have the poems copied and use them as my primary examples.

Revision

> Revision means re-seeing, re-visioning, hence re-thinking one's thoughts, over and again, to discover and clarify final meaning: the What-to-write and the How-to-write-it.
>
> — Joseph I. Tsujimoto (1984, 52)

Most student writings are egregiously flawed because students, never having been taught, do not know how to revise their work. Revision, for most students, is nothing more than tedious recopying, the penalty exacted for incorrect spelling, punctuation, and grammar. Revision, in this sense, yields little or no real improvement in their writing.

The game the students try to play is Get-it-right-the-first-time-through. The way they do that is to get, first of all, a good idea, as though *getting* good ideas means plucking them out of a tree. But (often at the last moment) pluck them they do — out of the proverbial Tree of Superficiality. With this as their modus operandi, is it any wonder that their writing lacks originality? That their writing fails to improve from one week to the next or throughout a semester?

The way we can help students become better writers is to cultivate in them the *capacity to suspend closure on the selection of a problem.*

We can do this by showing them the workable options — the various revisionary operations — that allow for genuine reseeing, that will lead them to problems worth addressing, problems that they themselves have discovered. Obviously, then and only then are the problems worth solving, worthy of the commitment that good writing demands.

The following revisionary options are variations on three of the eleven strategies I listed in "Re-Visioning the Whole" (Tsujimoto 1984).

Partner Revision

As Peter Elbow points out in *Writing with Power,* revision is most easily learned by working on someone else's writing. Free of the writer's preconceptions and biases for the poem, the reviser has an easier time making changes in the poem. That is, revising other people's work nurtures in the reviser the cold calculation necessary when reseeing, judging, and recasting their own work.

After exchanging drafts, parners revise the poems, on a separate page, as if the drafts were their own. What students want in return, I suggest, is not necessarily a second draft superior to the original, but a second draft that is markedly different from the original, that allows them to resee their work meaningfully. For it is in acknowledging, comparing, judging, and choosing among alternatives that the students learn how to improve their work.

In order to ensure second drafts that are markedly different from originals, I often assign partner revision in combination with revising by varying the audience, the speaker, the purpose, or the form of discourse. Or, if a particular area of concern arises, I will tell the students to revise their partners' work by focusing their attention on, perhaps, lining, spacing, and making stanzas, or on their suggesting new directions that the poem can take.

Students benefit not only from revising others' work and from the feedback gained through their partners' revisions, but also, as they have told me in their journals, from their partners' original drafts. They learn new vocabulary, new strategies of organization and possibilities of style, and bold new attitudes of tone and voice.

Revising by Group Feedback

The following approach is a modification of Elbow's revision groups. Students read their poetry twice to their group of four or five students. After the first reading, listeners write, on a scrap of paper, sentences in response to the following two questions: What do you think is the poem's central idea? What emotion, if any, does the poem arouse in you? After the second reading, the listeners write in response to two further questions: What words and phrases stuck in your mind because of their effectiveness? What would you work on if the poem were yours? Then the listeners give the author feedback orally before handing him or her their written responses. Since the responses are not threatening, emphasizing their subjectivity and demanding no esoteric knowledge of criticism, both the writer and listeners are disarmed by the positive nature of the comments.

Later, the authors can focus the group's attention by asking their own questions. By this time they know the kind of feedback that is needed, and suspect or sense where the poem may be weak.

Circle Revision

First, writers number their lines and attach a blank page to their original poem. Second, seated in a circle, they pass their originals to the reader on the left, who responds by choosing lines, by number, to revise on the attached page. Third, since everyone will not complete the work simultaneously, readers who finish early are to exchange papers with other students who have also completed their first revisions. The process continues in this manner, with each student working at a comfortable pace, until the class has produced multiple feedback for each poem.

After the initial exchange, subsequent readers also have the responsibility of responding to the alternative lines suggested by previous readers. If readers agree with the alternatives, they write "Yes." If they disagree, they can write "Keep Original," or they can write another alternative line.

Guidelines for Revision

I focus the students' attention on three areas of concern, sometimes separately, sometimes in combination. In the first area, *diction*, I suggest that students make verbs more vivid and forceful, make nouns more specific or precise, replace clichés and trite statements with statements that express the unique experience conveyed in the poem, and change dull, abstract statements into sensual "pictures," using imagery or tropes.

Regarding the second area, *compression*, I instruct students to delete redundant or ineffective words, to delete words that do not contribute information or that overload lines, to delete irrelevancies that dilute emotional impact, and to replace word groups with shorter expressions that do the same job with greater economy.

In the third area of revision, *development and extension,* students are to add words that supply the *who, where, when, how, why, whose,* or *which* where necessary for clarity and in places where ambiguity seems counterproductive to the poem's overall scheme; to add words at important points that seem to beg elaboration, and to add words or stanzas to the end of the poem, extending its possibilities and perhaps making the poem more original.

As with other feedback used for revision, none of the alternatives need be adopted. It is more important that writers be directed to areas that they themselves can improve, areas, for example, that inspire unanimous or controversial responses.

Evaluation

I wonder if you wanted to address the subject of poetry evaluation. Too subjective? Too banal?!!

— Richelle Fujioka (teacher, high school)

Would you consider touching this tough problem? How much does the teacher advise, suggest to the poet about "lining"? . . . In short, how much does the teacher "tamper" with the poems through pointed questions? . . . Indeed, 'tis a ticklish question.

— Nellie McGloughlin (teacher, grades 5-8)

The teachers' questions are these: *How* should the teacher evaluate student poetry? *How much* should the teacher advise the students? As I imply throughout this book, I can only volunteer how one teacher goes about this work. Let me answer the questions this way.

First, the image of poetry, when it is thought of at all, tends to be perverted in two ways: through the belief that it is less than what it is and through the belief that it is more than what it is. At the first extreme, poetry (like art in general) is shoved into the "creativity corner" by many administrators who pretend to champion its importance at awards assemblies and parent-teacher meetings. In general, it is deemed (again like the other arts) a divine gift given to the few, an idiosyncratic endeavor, or a frivolous waste of time. In English, not to mention the other disciplines, thinking that poetry writing is exclusively, and pejoratively, a creative endeavor can lead to the belief that the "more scholarly" endeavor of essay writing requires no creativity, as if creativity were not the chief cause of the first-rate essay or first-rate thinking. This negatively affects the way the essay is perceived by students and taught by teachers.

At the other extreme, where the perversion of poetry may be equally damaging, is the belief that poetry is somehow more precious than the other arts, more precious than music and painting, more precious than dance and drama, more precious than its cousins the short story, the personal narrative, and the essay. For some reason — according to some students, some parents, and even some teachers — criticizing a student's poem is tantamount to sacrilege, for by doing so, we dampen the poet's enthusiasm and inhibit budding creativity; worse, we condition the student to our understanding of excellence. To tamper with the poet's work is taboo. And to pronounce it shoddily done is justification to bear the umbrage and wrath of the poet's offended parents, who are not infrequently college graduates and professors.

Such consequences are rare, however, where the instructor corrects the beginning pianist, criticizes the novice ballerina, or gives advice to the fledgling painter, architect, or essayist. Like poetry, these arts are a craft to be mastered; they must be practiced, corrected, refined.

Part of the reason, I think, that poetry seems something exceptional compared to the other arts is that originally it was divinely inspired. Holy. The poet, then, was priest, seer, prophet, wise man, shaman — the mystic voice that enunciated the words of God. Such an age with such conviction, of course, has passed, and with its passing, the purity and holiness that was once without became, through time, attached to group and then to individual identity. Therefore, to comment on another's poetry is to comment on the poet's identity or personality, which is an unfortunate misunderstanding.

The corollary is this: in order to preserve and sustain selfhood, the poet must always work alone, independent of and beholden to no one, which is patently absurd because it is impossible. Not discounting Ezra Pound's advice to T. S. Eliot and other poets in their youth; Maxwell Perkin's advice to Hemingway, Fitzgerald, and Thomas Wolfe; or Ford Maddox Ford's advice to Conrad over *Heart of Darkness* — poets, whether or not influenced directly, are never alone, keeping their visions all to themselves.

Hamlet said, "there is nothing either good or bad, but thinking makes it so." That is, to answer the first teacher's questions — no, evaluation is not banal. It is a fact of life. Rather than moral relativity, Hamlet refers to the judgment born of thinking, defining the basically moral nature of humanity (however much Hamlet himself often wishes not to think).

Student poetry is good or bad insofar as it measures up to the best of the literary tradition that the students themselves have established (as in chapter 3 of this book), and insofar as it measures up to the best work a student has done to date, demonstrating growth or the lack thereof. More specifically, if the work shows growth, the poem demands comment (even if the work is graded a 2 in a 4-point system). "Getting stronger" is not an uncommon accompaniment to a grade. Otherwise, I say nothing about the work in general, speaking instead, in shorthand, about specific words, lines, and stanzas.

In answering the second teacher's question, I give the student as much advice as I can. What I mean by advice is for the teacher to suggest changes; to offer alternative words and means, asking the student to compare them with what the student has written; to ask the student to expand or compress, deepen or extend thoughts and feelings — that is, the teacher does exactly what the student revisers do. The difference between the teacher's subjective responses and those of the students (as well as those of lay adults) is that the teacher's subjectivity is born of specialized experience and training, which makes a great difference. Were I to withhold from my students my expertise — my critical opinion — I would have to call myself to account as a teacher who believes that by my actions, my students come to share, in part, my reverence for writing and literature.

Poetry Books

> It wasn't until the pages had covers on them that I knew I had written a book. Me! Sure, you feel kind of proud when the teacher puts your poem up for a week or reads it to the class but that's nothing like holding your own book in your hands. It's like holding all your clay sculptures in your hands at one time and saying this is what I did.
>
> — unknown student

Three things come to mind when I think of another favorite teacher, Professor Kriegel. The first is his shoot-from-the-hip responses to my short story characters, who, for the most part, tended toward loud, ignorant pronouncements on famous writers. ("One would wonder why that ass Fitzgerald bothered to write in the first place!")

A number of good things resulted from Kriegel's heavy-handed forthrightness. For one, my "vision" improved; I began to "see" more honestly. For another, I eventually published two works that had taken seed in his class. (One story, which was not published, was about him — only my hero was a heroine, a tyrannical virtuoso singer confined to a wheelchair. Her correspondence to Kriegel was uncanny and obvious, so obvious that I didn't recognize it until twelve years later.)

Second, and more important, I remember Kriegel's intolerance of mediocrity. This was evidenced not so much in his words as it was in his voice, in his street-fighter's grimace (which was his smile), and in his thick upper body that challenged you and hoped that you would do your best — that to do otherwise was dishonesty. His passion was infectious.

The third thing that comes to mind when I think of Kriegel is this: after setting his battered briefcase on the desk at the head of the class and propping his crutches against the chalk rail behind him, he bent to shift his steel-braced legs beneath the desk. On this particular day, he withdrew a book from his briefcase — his book, which had been published. He remarked, without raising his eyes, that there were a number of sentences or passages that he didn't recall writing. In any case, his talk was short, and we turned to our own work, though I'm sure others, like myself, watched him, fascinated. Oblivious to us, he seemed to fondle the book with his large powerful hands, feeling the spine, tracing its edges, testing the thickness and quality of the paper. Cradling the book in one hand, he flipped through the pages with the other, his eyes glazed with a fiercely possessive, fiercely proud light.

And so, after writing twenty-six poems, after arranging them in book form, after magically receiving them, spiral-bound, from the school's production center, my students have their own books to feel in their palms, to hold between their fingers. Yes, the books are real — the record of a whole quarter's effort, the proud product of what one student called "Mission Impossible, day after day."

As I return the books to them, in a very businesslike manner, I watch the students out of the corner of my eye. A few, as show, flip their books casually on their desks; others quickly glance at the pages, perhaps for publishing errors, while others want to see the books of their friends: "Let me see, let me see"; "Wow, this is thick"; "You sure wrote a lot"; "Boy, you write neatly." The room is filled with a loud, excited hum, which is colored, infused, and shaped by a sense of culmination, of having grown, of having arrived as expected. No big thing, really. Just a fact of life.

At the end of class, the books are hauled off to the closed reserve section of the library, where they are preserved fingerprint-free until Christmas vacation. At that time the books are returned to the students, who wrap them at home to give away as gifts to parents and grandparents. And how do *they* react? One common parent practice, according to my students (to my students' "chagrin"), is their having the book copied and sent, hither and yon, to the rest of the clan. Another practice is the parents telling me how surprised they are at the sophisticated level of their children's insight, their sensitivity, their emotional honesty — surprised, really, at the invisible, inner growth their children are experiencing, the growth of hearts and minds so close to their own yet never seen in this light before. And they are moved as only parents can be.

Each of the student books concludes with an End Poem (chapter 3, assignment number 18). The following poem, modeled on Jack Spicer's "Five Words for Joe Dunn on His 22nd Birthday," was written by Sam Onaga (grade 8).

A Christmas Present

For Christmas day
I give you
What I have
Five names.

Breug and his bronzed arms
Which are like soft walls
To brace you
From falls
And weather your blows.
For you;

Trink and his wit of chimes
To entertain you
With rainbow leaps
And shiny tinklings
During your long moments;

Schnook
The cynic
And his curled lip
To keep you thinking
In idle times;

Unk and his stupidity
And stumbling clumsiness
To laugh at
In bad times;
There is always one worse;

And *Is-Was*
His twinkling eyes and reverent speech
To remind you
To make you look back and remember
When you can't look forward.

3 Poems and Poetry Assignments

It is as though the poem gave the reader as he left it a single, new *word* never before spoken and impossible to actually enunciate, but self-evident as an active principle in the reader's consciousness henceforward.

— Hart Crane (1966, 221)

1. Found Poem

1. Copy one or two unique, rich, musical, or odd sentences found in a newspaper, magazine, history book, encyclopedia, letter, and so forth.

2. Break the sentences into poetic lines, arranging words and phrases in the most meaningful and surprising ways.

3. a. Title your work Found Poem.

   b. Beneath your title write (in parentheses) "words from" title of article (in quotes), title of publication (underlined), date, page number.

   c. At the end of your poem, and to the right, write "— arranged by" your name.

Found Poem

(words from "Food Report," <u>Honolulu Advertiser,</u>
September 1982, p. 1)

Pasta ranges,
In shape,
From the strand,
Of spaghetti,
To the butter-
Fly-like
Farfalle,
To the penne pasta.
And,
It ranges,
In size,

From the bird-
Shot-
Like acini
De pepe,
To the large,
Tube,
Called,
Mani-
Cotti.

— arranged by David Liao
(grade 8)

I don't know who originated the Found Poem assignment, but it has been floating around for years from teacher to teacher, text to text. It is an ingenious assignment used to introduce students to lining and spacing, without their having the burden of also inventing their own words. Here the students may play and experiment with a variety of strategies, seeing for themselves how array affects meaning, how the deployment of the given words alters the cumulative meaning originally intended by the prose sentence.

In contrast to the sentence in prose, the basic unit of meaning in a poem is the line, which may be constituted of a single word or even a particle of a word. The line not only means what it means as it is "defined" by the sentence in which it appears — a sentence that may span a number of lines, as David's two sentences do — but the line can also assert its own meaning. "Pasta ranges" suggests that the pasta moves, is active, has a life of its own. It is like "butter, "butter-/Fly-like," "Fly-like," like a "bird," "bird-/Shot-/Like," and like a "tube." In breaking sentences into their particles and grouping the particles in lines, David has transformed prose into poetry. In this particular instance, using the same number of words, David has created meanings in addition to those established by the grammar of the sentences. If we transform the lines back to prose sentences, the music of the words will be dampened, the colors and pictures will fade, and the words — self-sufficient in the poem — will become dependent again upon other words, other sentences, for their significance. Something uncommon will become dramatically less so.

Pasta ranges in shape from the strand of spaghetti to the butterfly-like farfalle to the penne pasta. And it ranges in size from the birdshot-like acini de pepe to the large tube called manicotti.

Preparing students for this assignment, I first write the following sentences and their poetic versions on the blackboard. (A poet-teacher friend had sent me this exercise years ago.)

> My brother is an animal lover, sometimes hater. Sometimes he likes to shout, Get a horse, Help, Air, Clear out!

Poem A

My brother is
an animal lover
sometimes hater
sometimes he likes to shout
Get a horse
Help   Air   Clear out!

Poem B

My brother is an animal
Lover, sometimes
Hater, sometimes
He likes to shout
Get a horse
Help
Air
Clear Out!

I read the poems aloud once and then read them again, observing the following points, though not always all the points, nor in the same order:

1. Poetry is written differently than prose. In a poem, how the words are arranged affects their meaning. Compare the first three lines of Poem A to the first three lines of Poem B. In Poem A, the brother is a lover and a hater *of animals.* In Poem B, the brother is three general things: an animal, a lover, and a hater.

2. How the words are arranged determines how we read the words. Compare the rhythm and pace of the last two lines of Poem A to the last four lines of Poem B. Poem A's words are read rapid-fire, while Poem B's words are read more slowly, distinctly. Also, when reading lines that do not end with punctuation, we make the slightest of pauses. For example, in Poem A the "is" in "My brother is" is given greater stress than the "is" in "My brother is an animal."

3. The end of a line is a prominent position, where poets often place words they wish to emphasize. Compare "My brother is" to "My brother is an animal." In the former, "is" emphasizes the brother's undeniable existence, as well as the undeniability of the facts that follow; in the latter, "animal" suggests that the brother is something less than human.

4. One of the pleasures of reading poetry is being surprised. One obvious way that poets try to surprise us is through their choice of words and phrases, or lines. The opening line of Poem B surprises us with its bluntness. In both poems, "Get a horse" is surprising because it is a rare expression, as "Air" might be, given the other exhortations. A second way poets try to surprise us is by altering, inverting, or shortening the usual ways things are expressed in writing. The second and third lines of Poem B, "Lover, sometimes/Hater, sometimes," drop both subjects and verbs, if we accept them as sentences. A third way poets try to surprise us is through the movement between lines, forcing us to shift our bearings, even if only slightly. Line five of Poem A, "Get a horse," surprises us in a subtle way, since we anticipate another of the brother's characteristics to be added to the list, which the poem has been thus far.

5. Both poems omit punctuation in the shaping of their separate meanings. Poem B, on the other hand, includes a comma in line three, making the grammar of line three identical to line two. You, too, may add or omit punctuation in the shaping of your own poems.

6. Capitalizing the first word of every line, as in Poem B, is an optional convention. You may only want to capitalize the first words of sentences or the first words of stanzas, or you might not want to capitalize any words at all. What will determine *all* your choices is your desire to communicate effectively your intended meanings.

7. None of this is to say poems A and B are great poems by any means, though they are, in fact, poems.

Then I shift my observations to spacing.

1. We could separate lines five and six of Poem A from the preceding lines, making two stanzas (say for the purpose of making "Get a horse" more surprising):

. . . .
Sometimes he likes to shout

Get a horse
Help   Air   Clear out!

Stanzas often indicate changes: of steps in a progression, of forms of discourse (as above), of subject, of attitude, of time or place, of perspective, of focus, of point of view, of speaker, and so forth.

2. Sometimes poets emphasize words by separating them from other words in a line through extra spaces. Poem B could end

Help
Air
Clear   Out!

Separation here would slow our reading, emphasizing further the brother's meaning. Or we could end with a one-word stanza (nearly separating "Clear Out!" and giving "Clear" nearly as much "value" as the preceding exclamations):

Help
Air
Clear

Out!

3. Note the addition and omission of spacing in the Found Poem by Laura Marceau (grade 9):

Found Poem

It
can be Misty
Gray
or
Brilliant White.
Clouds
Closeinbriefly
then
part   like   veils
Sometimes
when rain stains the stone,
You'll hear
A visitor say,

"Doesn't it look
as
if
they're
c
  r
    y
      i
        n
          g
           ?"

4. You may also omit words. In the first of the two examples shown
   below, Rebecca Gelber (grade 8) omits the word "and" — indi-
   cated by the ellipsis — creating irony:

Found Poem
(words from *National Geographic*,
September 1985, p. 282)

Cassette Recorders
HUGE
as suitcases
blARE **O   U   T**
Hong Kong
love songs
. . . English
lessons

Brian Furuno (grade 8) omits many words from his poem, making
the narrative portion of the poem conform dialectically to the
quoted words at the end. Though he does not indicate through
ellipses all the places he has omitted words, his decision, in this
instance, seems apropos of his wry intentions.

Found Poem
(words from *National Geographic*,
August 1984, p. 261)

The Puffer,
Blowfish, Swellfish,
or in Japanese,
the Fugu.

Eating the Fugu in Japan?
$200 for four.

But the Fugu
Perhaps
the world's most deadly fish.

The poison
of the Fugu
A terrible death!
Arms,
Legs,
become numb.
You can think
but cannot move
and soon
Cannot breathe . . .

> "Last night he and I ate Fugu;
> Today, I help carry his coffin."

Though the above information may appear too much to cover in a class period, it is not. Since I do the "observing," and I don't expect them to assimilate everything, it takes less than twenty minutes to point these ideas out. My concern is the next ten minutes, where they practice lining the following sentences:

> I am returning this book about mystery over women which I borrowed ten days ago. Unfortunately, my wife wouldn't let me keep it.

After a few minutes, four or five students write their poetic versions on the board. Then we discuss the variety of new meanings and effects that have been created because of the strategies the writers have employed — teaching, again, some of the options available to them.

Several examples of students' Found Poems follow.

Found Poem
(words from *Honolulu Star Bulletin*)

There is
a definite aristocracy
in the
world
of nuts.

The best-known walnuts . . .
are the English.
Which have a far more
crackable . . .
Shell,
than the black.

Looks
can be
deceiving —

— arranged by Rosalyn Won
(grade 8)

Found Poem
(words from "Sunday Cartoons,"
Honolulu Bulletin & Advertiser)

You
    heavy
metal
    meatheads
and Madonna Wanna-Bees
We're going to learn about
    Abstract Art
    today

Here's a painting by
    The GREAT Pablo Gookman . . .
feel the urban confusion
and sense the t
                    w
                i
                    s
                t
                    e
                d   cityscape.
you can almost taste the
    blackened soot of backstreet garbage
in gutters of . . . of . . . decaying
    ROT
Gookman's title seems to have escaped me.
WILL someone look it up?

It's called,
            "A Pink Snow Bunny"

                                    — arranged by Caryn Nakamura
                                    (grade 8)

2. Two-Word Poem

1. Make three poems, each constituted of two concrete nouns. The first word of each poem is the "subject," which the second word describes by suggesting similarity.

2. Avoid word combinations that suggest cause and effect, object and action, object and quality, object and environment.

3. Title your works Poem I, Poem II, Poem III, to indicate to your audience that your words are to be read as poetry.

            Hands

                        birds

                        — Mary Caroline Richards

I write this two-word poem by Richards on the board. Students are quickly led to understand that we read the poem according to the conventions of English, left to right, top to bottom, and according to the convention of reading similes: "Hands" are like "birds."

For the next five minutes students brainstorm on their own the characteristics of different birds, all the things they do, and how they do these things. Then I ask: In what ways are hands like birds? They respond: Hands are soft like a dove, and graceful too, especially in hula, swaying and gliding through the air, and swooping on their prey, ripping out its heart with a beak, but some are shy and timid, nervous too, you see them shaking in the rainy cold, or scratching — my sister has long sharp nails, talons, my sister paints hers orange, or yellow like webbed feet, or a bill, my cousin has lips like a bill, talks like a duck, hands talk in a way, steal things too, sly birds, birds are always hungry, they eat all day making a mess everywhere, well, people are like that. And so forth.

Then I read Pound to them: *Great literature is simply language charged with meaning to the utmost degree* (1960, 36). I talk about spacing and the unexplainable "rightness" of Richards's arrangement — how, if we were to alter the position of her words, the poem's impact would be made less effective, less natural, affecting its sense of "flight." For example, none of the following would do:

Hands   birds

                  Hands

birds

            Hands

            birds

Next we play Word Association Game I to exercise their association skills. There are only two rules: (1) barring obscenities, say the first thing that comes to mind as suggested by the given word and (2) try to make your responses specific and concrete, as "sea urchin" would be in response to "porcupine." The teacher repeats "porcupine" (or another object word), for each student, moving rapidly around the room. Students may say "Pass" if they wish. After a couple of rounds, the teacher can field responses as the ideas occur to the students. Stop only to commend those who offer unusual responses, as "boot polish" would be to "porcupine," pointing out the color parallel between the two. Such emphases encourage others to see in terms of a thing's characteristics or attributes, expanding the number and kinds of ways that they can "see." The game compels them to think of likenesses and connections between apparently dissimilar things, fostering new discoveries. This is the direction we want them eventually to take in playing with ideas. Besides, the game is frantic and fun, tapping unconscious knowledge that the mind, under academic pressure, suppresses.

Next I write ten or twelve student examples on the board; then we talk about our favorites. Among mine are the following four poems:

Cathedral

Cascade

— Fritz Johnson (grade 8)

Fritz's poem captures for me the glittering whiteness and shadow of a waterfall descending over a steep, rocky surface, or a series of waterfalls sparkling and gauzy and shimmering — like the light shimmering over the fretwork of a Gothic facade, creating a luminescent haze. Had Fritz seen one or more of Monet's twenty paintings of Rouen Cathedral? No matter. His vision is impeccably "right." "Waterfall" or "Cataract," instead of "Cascade," would never do.

Legsfrogs

— Anissa Arquette (grade 8)

When Anissa first wrote her poem, the *L, f,* and the two *g*'s were elongated lines that looked like legs. Her poem reminded me of an ideogram, just a step before becoming a complex character in Oriental writing, or just before separating into discrete words found in the West.

PENCIL SHARPENER

ANTEATER

— Caren Wun (grade 8)

Caren's poem affects me in odd ways. The shape of the objects are approximate, especially if one puts a pencil into the mouth of the sharpener. Its long snout? In addition, the sharpener "eats" small things. Caren makes an inanimate thing curiously alive.

Grandmother

Porcelain

— Mindy Starn (grade 8)

Mindy's poem evokes for me embroidered antimacassars draped on the arms and backs of heavy, overstuffed furniture; tea cups, standing lamps, dried flowers, clocks, yarn, frugality, jellied mints, peanut brittle, brussels sprouts, tarnished oval mirrors, thin carpets, spectacles resting on an open Bible in the woolen snugness of a parlor, late afternoon. A whole world, now gone, arises before my mind's eye, and for a moment I am transported, reunited with my past.

Additional examples of students' Two-Word Poems follow.

Poem IV

Gyroscope

pulley

—Ricky Kakazu (grade 7)

Poem

Autumn

Punk Rock

— Garrett Suehiro (grade 7)

Poem III

Spiderweb

Magnet

— Jennifer Davis (grade 8)

Poem I
Ember
    Marigold

            — Kerri Ting (grade 8)

Poem II
Television
      Mesmerist

            — Brian Jim (grade 8)

Poem I
Lion
Tuba

            — Brent Matsumoto (grade 7)

Poem
Scarecrow   Crucifix

            — Brady Onishi (grade 8)

Poem III
hacksaw
    piranha

            — Rosalyn Won (grade 8)

Poem
Childhood

Musicbox

            — Tai Fyrberg (grade 8)

3. Circle Poem

1. Write a poem where your title "triggers" the word or phrase of your first line, which, in turn, "triggers" the next line, and so forth.

2. Try to surprise us with each new line, taking us each time to a new world — taking us on a rich, various trip through time, place, ideas, objects, colors, tastes, names, and so forth.

3. Your poem will end when your last line "circles" back to the beginning, approximating your title.

Snow Tracks

Bird madness
*
Petroglyphs
*
Tombstones
*
Stonehenge
*
The Great Wall
*
Yin-Yang
*
Lost & Found
*
Wedding gown
*
No   Sound
*
Wet windowpane
*
Snowbound

As I mentioned in chapter 2, I wrote the above poem in order to focus the students' attention on the poetic movement between lines. First, I lead them to their own interpretations about how the lines are linked:

"Snow Tracks" is linked to "Bird madness" through identification: criss-crossing bird tracks are imprinted in snow, their direction and meaning without apparent sense.

"Bird madness" is linked to "Petroglyphs" through imagery: petroglyphs are pictographs — stick figures and line symbols — inscribed in stone, which is hard like ice and cold like snow.

"Petroglyphs" is linked to "Tombstones" through "stone" and inscriptions on stone, like epitaphs, whose extinct authors belong to history.

"Tombstones" is linked to "Stonehenge" through "stone" and history, emphasizing the passage of time; Stonehenge was an enormous solar calendar constructed of huge upright stones laid out, like a clock, on the Salisbury Plain in Wiltshire, England, built by the ancient Druids, an ephemeral race.

"Stonehenge" is linked to "The Great Wall" of China through "stone" and longevity. The 2,000-mile wall was erected in the third century B.C. to wall out the nation's enemies: barbarians, history — and time?

"The Great Wall" is linked to "Yin-Yang" through heritage. In Chinese philosophy and religion, the Yin and the Yang represent two principles: the Yin is associated with the negative and the feminine; the Yang is associated with the positive and the masculine, whose traits exist in proportion in both sexes, whose complements exist in others. The interaction of the two principles in human relationships influences the destiny of people.

"Yin-Yang" is linked to "Lost & Found" through the likeness of pairs that suggest opposition and complementation. "Lost" suggests loss and death, while "Found" denotes recovery, most often of an object lost in time.

"Lost & Found" is linked to "Wedding gown" through rhyme and grammar. "Wedding gown" is the implied object of the verbs "Lost & Found." However, though the object may be recovered, the life attached to it, now lost, cannot. We know a life has been lost because of the poem's "grammar," whose subject, for the most part, is the past, the dead, the extinct — what is found in memory.

"Wedding gown" is linked to "No   Sound" by rhyme and by the way of cause and effect. The discoverer of the wedding gown — the speaker, the persona — is rendered speechless; and that speechlessness, at the same time, speaks with the pathos and tragedy common to a Noh play, which is full of "Sound," however melancholy.

"No   Sound" triggers "Wet windowpane," the sudden consciousness of immediate place, as the eyes focus on the object nearest at hand. The window is wet because of internal condensation.

"Wet windowpane" leads to the original setting beyond the window, as consciousness widens, deepens. The setting now is reinterpreted as "Snowbound," having been influenced by the speaker's reverie, his train of thought, his memory. The speaker feels isolated, alone.

Obviously, my students and I don't speculate at such length. It is enough that we invent reasonable links: that is the focus.

Next we play Word Association Game II, in which the teacher initiates the train of class thought by giving the first student a word, say "pagoda." Then in quick succession around the classroom, students react to the preceding word, phrase, or sentence. "Pagoda," "Japan," "Tokyo," "Hiroshima," "atomic bomb," "Vietnam," "World War III" is a possible train of thought. Here, the teacher stops to commend those who make associative leaps, bypassing obvious or trite intermediary steps in a progression ("Japan," "Tokyo"), choosing instead "conclusions" that create unique sequences of thought ("pagoda," "Treblinka," "atomic bomb"). The teacher also stops to commend those who make leaps that redirect the train of thought, as "calculus" would in response to "World War II" or as "topaz" or "arbor" would in response to "Pearl Harbor."

Often, part of the class will be stuck on a subject or a place or a predictable progression. In such instances, as though in physical pain, I groan, "Boring. . . . Can anyone get us out of the department store?" They all laugh. After all, it is a game. (The juniors and seniors I taught at Seabury Hall on Maui used to play the word association game at parties to test each other on emotional issues, like sex, friends, school, money — especially sex. And I was amazed at the ingenious escape devices they invented off-the-cuff under pressure . . . to the chagrin and disappointment of the group.)

What we are looking for is the unexpected shift, the surprise leap, to another mental-emotional world, exercising alternative ways of thinking in addition to logic. Just what we want in poetry — poems that make us see anew.

Again and again I refer the students to the Circle Poem — the short stanzas that they themselves have created — in order to remind them of the infinite possible progressions that poetry can accommodate. That is, think of the Circle Poem; think of your stanzas as single words; and think of the leaps you made from "word" to "word."

Examples of students' Circle Poems follow.

Chicken

afraid
height
Empire State Building
King Kong
Curious George
yellow
fall
break
dance
canteen
water

sky
Henny Penny

— Dana Cargill (grade 7)

Lovesong

One dance
Carousel
Music Box
Memories
Photograph
Glass Image
Stranger
Razor Blade
Sirens

— Sandra Kim (grade 8)

Vikings

Scandinavia
*
snow
*
white
*
elves
*
magic
*
night
*
owl
*
wise
*
man
*
primates
*
orangutan
*
red
*
autumn
*
Leif

— Calvin Nii (grade 8)

4. Change Poem

1. Write a poem describing a single change or multiple changes using one-word lines and stanzas.

2. The changes you show — as you had shown in your Circle Poem — should be unpredictable and surprising. However, for this poem, your changes should show leaps through time.

3. Note that the sample Change Poems are primarily events.

First, the class reads and discusses several student examples, to identify and consider rhetorical devices that they can exploit and to list general topics under which they will later brainstorm specific topics.

One common topic is the change of season.

> Autumn
>
> Dead
> Leaves
> Flutter
> Like
> Butterflies
>
> To
> The
> Ground
>
> Red
> Orange
> Brown
>
> Spreading
> Out
> Like
> A
> Sheet
> Of
> Ice

> — unknown student (grade 8)

By the last stanza winter takes hold: glittering colors, "leaves," and "butterflies" are held captive by "Spreading . . . Ice," or "flutter," fade, and die, their *faces* covered by a cold, white "Sheet." The first simile vivifies the leaves, while the second implies both temporary and permanent change.

Mosquito

Squirming
worms
in
a
puddle
they're
gone
you
scratch
your
head.

— Keli Sato (grade 7)

The change in the poem above is almost instantaneous, as is the wonderful experience of irony. Suddenly "we" itch after something, while we laugh. A physical transformation, physical movements, and a change of mood or state of mind combine to produce "simple" poetry, powerful enough to light up our faces.

Brown Bagged

Fresh
Brown
Wholewheat

Meat
Wet
With
Condiments

Droopy
And
Old

Salmonella

— Laura Murray (grade 7)

I can picture the student opening her lunch sack, unwrapping her sandwich, and inspecting its content with tentative forefinger and thumb. Often have I felt my sandwiches diseased, and I have gone without.

Student poems address other things that rot, grow corrupt, or decompose.

Nephew

At
first
nice
quiet

Then
learning
to
talk

To
be
a
nuisance

Now
serving
time
without
parole

— Satoshi Hayasaka (grade 7)

Legs

Tiny
and
weak

then
cutely
chubby

skinny

now
bigger
stronger.

Oh
yuck

Fat!

— Brooke Wilmeth (grade 7)

The second poem, "Legs," at first seems obvious, trite, tedious even —
until the last stanza when (surprise!) a person speaks: disappointed,
disgusted, discovering her expectation undercut at fruition. Suddenly

a personal poem becomes universal, and we laugh. In any case, one thing we can say is that people change eventfully.

Metamorphosis

First,
a
cell
exploding.

Next,
a
slithery
blob,
darting
nervously.

Now,
a
bungling
tadpole
trudging
through
murky
sands.

Finally,
a
dignified
frog,
springing
onto
lilypads;
croaking
arrogantly,
its
nose
in
the
air.

— Laura Marceau (grade 9)

Using a frog and its development to maturity, the writer of "Metamorphosis" uses extended metaphor to comment on human devel-

opment, which often culminates in loud, presumptuous self-impor-
tance, especially in the eyes of sensitive teenagers.

Bus

A
Bit
Squeaky
Otherwise
Quiet
Empty

Full
Of
Fresh
Air

Then
Gets
Stuffy

Noisey
Full

Of
Candywrappers
Papers

Footprints
Graffiti

A
Cut
Seat

Groans
While
Chugging
Along

— Lisa Nakamura (grade 7)

In the fifth stanza, Lisa's poem leaps in time over people to what
they have done, undercutting our expectation. The last stanzas per-
sonify the bus as it groans under its heavy load and through the groan
of the wounded seat — suggesting the thoughtless and sometimes
malicious changes we perpetrate on things . . . and others.

5. Transformation Poem

1. Write a poem describing a worker becoming a part, a tool, or a product of his or her work. This requires your intimate knowledge of the particular work process and the attitudes, responsibilities, and language connected to the work.

2. Do not use any form of the following words: become, change, transform. *Instead, make us experience the transformation.*

> The Seamstress
>
> is a hardy old woman
> with pins
> sticking
> out of her mouth.
>
> Thread in hand
> with a needle
> She
> bastes
> hems
> appliques
> a Raggedy Ann.
>
> Her face —
> an old wrinkled pincushion
> pins stuck in her painted mouth
> two black buttons for eyes
> hair of fine vermillion thread.
>
> — Julie Lim (grade 8)

After I read the assignment and several examples to the students, the class brainstorms various kinds of work people do, beginning with their parents' occupations and hobbies and moving to the kinds of work they have done themselves. I write their contributions on the board as they shout the suggestions to me. After they agree on one form of work, they brainstorm again under three categories: Verbs for Work, Tools of Work, and Products of Work. Then, under the students' direction, I write their lines for a class Transformation Poem — usually about an exterminator who becomes a cockroach. (One class wrote a poem about a bus driver who, after running over a dog, bends over the carcass and begins mangling its neck.)

Though the class is loud and seems chaotic, the experience is clearly inspiring, as students simultaneously and effusively volunteer opinions, wrangle over words and lines, and compromise on commas, as possessive as hens, as finicky as cats.

In any case, this sense of serious play is carried over into students' poetic endeavors at home, as demonstrated in the Transformation Poems that follow.

Lion Tamer

In a cage
he cracks the
floor with his whip.
Backing off huge
ferocious lions.

At 5 o'clock
he rushes home beat and weary.

He finds his impatient wife waiting.
She taunts him like a school teacher
about his tardiness.
He grabs a stool
and backs her off.

— Tim Dang (grade 7)

Tombstone

The gravedigger
teeters on the edge of the grave,
as he peers down at the rotting,
oak casket.

He picks up a shovel
and spoons soil
into the cavity.

Stamping his feet,
he packs the dirt.

His job done,
he mops his brow,
and sits on the freshly turned sod,

His aching body hardening
into
stone.

— Mindy Starn (grade 8)

Sketching

The frazzled cartoonist
sips his coffee thoughtfully

He seizes a pen and begins
to doodle everything that
comes to him

He selects a picture that
he likes and stares at
it, the characters' images
sticking to his brain

Hours pass, and no punch
line comes to him. Frustrated,
he animates his body and
walks toward his bedroom
frame by frame, muttering
to himself in word balloons

— Trevor Williamson (grade 8)

The Banker

little squarish man
probing for assets
carefully collecting money
rarely lending it,

locking all his secrets
within the confines of his soul
currency forever secured inside

with only himself to view it,
        SAFE . . .

— Josh Peters (grade 8)

Terrorist

He waits in the cheap
motel for the call that will summon him

The phone rings and a grim
smile flickers across his face. Calmly
dressed as a businessman he leaves
for the airport.

He stands in a ticket line alert
and ready. Then in an instant he
pulls out a Mac-10 and riddles the
crowd with bullets making them spin
in their dance of death.

His eyes become scopes. Arms
become barrels. Chest becomes
a stock. Death follows wherever
he points. A machine made to
kill.

— Scott Mattoch (grade 8)

6. List of Twelve

1. Unless you wish to work alone, share your word lists with your partner; then choose one category in which the words are rich and suggestive. Together, write a poem based on those words.

2. Of course, you do not have to use all the words. On the other hand, you may add words for grammatical clarity. You may also borrow words from other people's lists.

Desert Terrain

The desert's irascibility
        is like a wool sweater
        on a scorching day,
        and pinching wooden clogs.

Irritable sands,
        gritty like a cat's tongue,
        like slipping on sidewalk,
        and abrasive cleansers.

Sandspurs cling like velcro,
        to the burning, tormenting winds.

Tumble weeds of steel wool,
        entwine on cactus splinters.

The barren waste erodes
        life,
                like a nail file.

— Ashley Maynard and
Mindy Starn (grade 8)

First, students brainstorm, for a minute each, on the following twelve topics, quickly listing all the words and phrases that come to mind. The teacher announces the topic and keeps track of the time.

1. The smell of gasoline
2. Cut with a knife
3. Saran Wrap
4. The smell of a book
5. Electric razor
6. Fish scales
7. Split pea soup
8. Crystal
9. Gong
10. Kissing
11. Sandpaper
12. Cracking knuckles

Then students pick partners, share their lists, choose a category, and choose words, organizing the work for the night.

The first time I assigned the List of Twelve (which I got from Paul Wood, a poet friend), I collected the students' lists, selected the most vivid words (making twelve lists), and had the lists duplicated for each student, to ensure their poems would be rich in diction. I should have been more confident in their judgment. In the last few years, they did just as well without the help of my lists; in fact, they did better drawing upon their own lists. But I am glad I bothered to collect and collate their words, for I can show you the kinds of words students tend to generate.

1. *The smell of gasoline:* blue-gray shirt, burn, stink, fluid, VW, orange, diesel, pink, lipstick, ethyl, tuna, skunk, black, ink, purple, aspirin, sewing machine, high, sick, Indian reservation, dizzy, socks, glue, sniff, snort, crazy, headrush, spaced-out, unleaded, fumes, flying, station, credit cards, Sears, grease, tires, flames, smoke, infection, gasping, oily, hood, engine, aquarium, wheel, Arabs, pump, attendant, tank, hot, coal, spill, truck, motorcycle, detergent, fur, license plate, explosion, carbon, tar, liquor, shabby

12. *Cracking knuckles:* snap, arthritis, cartilage, bones, disjoint fingers, nose, click, Yashica, dislocated, wood breaking, squeal, squirrel, old, knock, fracture, sprain, jam, ice, boxers, burglar, wrist, ankle, grandmother, bacon, peanut butter, brittle, hack, crackle, Ben Gay, crooked, double-jointedness, nerves, broken,

frogs, mousetrap, arm, beef, stamps, swell, popcorn, groan,
chills, think, Anacin, clack, thumb, stiffen, elbow, neck, toes,
pencils, walnut, karate, fire crackers, busting, pecking, hammer,
bent, habit, stretching, dad

The purpose of the List of Twelve assignment is to sensitize the
students to precise, vivid, vigorous words and to practice uniting words
into "families."

Examples of students' List of Twelve poems follow.

Remembrance of a Knuckle

The thighbone is connected to the
thigh
The fingerbone is connected to the
knuckle

The knuckle
I can remember those days
of cracking knuckles
The neat sound it made
like popcorn exploding
It was the thing back in those days
to see who could crack
the most knuckles

How I regret that I did that
I am 63 and overweight
I have arthritis
And it's very painful
The doctor said it's from
cracking my knuckles   but I
didn't believe him

Excuse me
Crack!
I still don't.

— Travis Otaguro and
Virginia Strevey (grade 8)

The Punchbowl

Salt from early morning surf
sparkles like diamonds

as the shining sun
rises above the mountain.

The beads of water
form clear geometric patterns
as the white wash
tumbles over the rocks.

As the quartz bell rings
I return to reality
discovering that the glittering light

is reflecting from the chandelier
and I am motionless before
the punchbowl filled with wine.

— unknown student (grade 7)

Split Pea Soup

My dad makes this soup every Sunday
he slurps it up with his
small red tongue.
His teeth clink against the spoon
which hits against the bowl.
Sometimes he puts on his garden gloves,
to pick the peas to make his own.
Then he pretends he is a cook,
places a large white hat on his head,
and sings while he makes
his gross dinner.
He adds all kinds of things,
mostly bad.
Peas as round as hippos
and crocodile greens.
Then he sits and eats alone,
shouting, "Anybody want some?"
We all scream!
So he goes back to eat his,
mushy green soup,
so messy his napkin looks like a swamp.

— Brooke Wilmeth and
Jessica Slater (grade 8)

Kissing

Kissing,
will be a dream
two sets of moist lips
meeting together
in a tender
        embrace

Brace?

My braces!

What if we lock?
It would be like
stepping on a leech
and trying to rip it off.

What if he's a frog,
with fat slug lips,
and a slimy tongue?

Feeling the saliva,
on his fish-sucking lips,
is bad enough.
        But what if I
taste his tongue!

GROSS

Kissing's hideous

— Whitnee Chun and
Allen Rice (grade 8)

7. Animal Poem

1. Write a poem about an animal or using an animal. You can describe the animal, talk to the animal, or be the animal, or you can use all three approaches.

2. Whatever your intentions, knowing the animal intimately — its habits, idiosyncracies, anatomy, habitat, diet, and so forth — should prove helpful to you. The library might help. Direct observation surely will.

The Baboon

You're half dog, half monkey.
You sit out of sight
Calmly out of sight
Then
As the roar of a car comes down the road
You move with your pack into its path.
Dust rises
As the car
Screeches to a halt
Your white and black fur
Glistens
In the sun
As you run and jump on the hood.
Then your dog-like face stares in at the people
You're curious.
And you try to look at them from every angle.
Is there anything to eat?
Lemon or orange peels?
Fruits?
Vegetables?
Sandwiches?
And as if that weren't enough
You kill and eat rabbits
Small buck
And rats
One blow of your massive paw means death
You sink your sharp teeth into your victim's skull
Cracking it
Then with your hands pull out the brains
You skin the poor thing
Pull it apart
Eating
Till finally, the lump of fur and blood no longer
        resembles the animal it once was
On all fours you disappear into the bush
Unknown

— Martin Griggs (grade 7)

After reading the above poem, I read several adult works and talk about the basic mystery of nature, human attitudes toward being and creation, and the poets' use of animals as a way of talking about other subjects.

Following "Baboon," I read the following poems:

Ted Hughes's "Hawk Roosting," where the hawk tells us his "manners are tearing off heads"

Blake's "The Lamb," which is about the innocence — sinlessness — of animals and children, and "The Tiger," whose speaker asks of the Tiger, "Did he who made the Lamb make thee?"

W. S. Merwin's "Leviathan," the awesome creature of the *deep* who "waits for the world to begin"

W. D. Snodgrass's "Lying Awake," whose speaker questions the moth's obsession for light as it climbs his "studypane"

Ted Hughes's "The Jaguar," whose "stride" — though physically caged in a monk's cell — "is wildernesses of freedom"

Yeats's "The Cat and the Moon," where the poet takes musical delight in their harmonious correspondence

Karl Shapiro's "The Fly," which begins, to the students' delightful disgust, "O hideous little bat, the size of snot" and which grows through six graphic stanzas, from decay and maggots, disease and amputation, human violence and hatred, until finally the Fly "dies between three cannibals." (After reading this poem at a high school assembly, I was deluged by requests for copies. Once, after reading this at camp, one eighth grader wanted to shake my hand!)

Finally, I read student examples, such as the following Animal Poems.

Ukus [cooties]

Clinging to the roots
Of you hair
Like periwinkles to rock

Like sand sticking
To your
Wet skin
They don't let go

They leap with joy
Having found a new
Head

Dandruff flakes, except alive
They swarm together
To party and play cards
Screaming, "Nits and lice are wild!"

— Laura Murray (grade 7)

Siamese Fighting Fish

The fish glides gracefully across the tank
His unblinking eyes stare bold and blank
His fantail flaps like a flag
Proud in his rainbow-plated armor
      he hovers majestically over a sea of gem-like gravel
Then, instinctively, it arches into a warrior's stance
With one swift movement it lunges at its prey
After viciously tearing it apart
      it feasts on its remains like a barbarian

— Jason Benn (grade 8)

Netherland Snails

Warm, firm hands clasp mine, as they
      keep me from stumbling
Over pebbles and clumps of
      hardened earth.
My mom and I walk through
      a deep green forest filled with
Stolid, leafy trees and stinging
      nettles.

As we walk along the fluffy, earthen-brown
      path,
We come to a low, crumbling
      stone wall — placed there
For the Great Snails.
      I gaze in wonder at them, as
Their slimy bodies with moist, pale skin,
      leave trails of shining paste
         as they ease patiently forward.

Their spiraling, calico shells rock
    slowly back and forth,
As the snails progress towards the
    wall's edge.
I touch one of the snail's antennae,
    and he sheathes them,
In shyness.

My mother's chafed, brown hands
    caress one of our regal friends,
    and lifts him into the cardboard box;
The snail withdraws into his shell,
    then peeks out cautiously.

My mom gathers a bundle of fresh, dewy
    grass, and tender pine needles
Still pale with youth.
    She places the pine-scented specks
    of green in the box
Trying not to disturb the snail.

I watch the mighty adult in
    wonder,
Her care-worn face looking
    cheerful now.
She notices me looking at her,
    and she smiles with her eyes warmly.
She points to the snail
    in the box.

I look, . . . see that the snail
    has crawled up the box's wall;
I look at my mother, and
    our eyes embrace.
She gingerly scoops the snail
    from the box, and places him on the wall.

                         — Kirstin Larson (grade 8)

8. Visual Response Poem

1. Write a poem about one of the reproductions — paintings or photographs — displayed on the chalk rail or taped to the walls.

2. *Comment on its details. What more can you "see," what more can you say?*

3. *Include the title and author of the work in your title.*

Andrew Wyeth's *Cristina's World*

She lies
cradled in a vast yellow brown sea
wearing a faded pink dress,
her dark hair
escaping
futile efforts
to confine it.

A lonely scene
surrounds her,
a rusty outline,
once, maybe,
a plow
or a wagon,
a gray house
weather-beaten,
worn by time,
blank window
staring.

She takes all of this in.
But in her mind,
this is no desolate tableau.
The house is recently built,
two horses pull a wagon and a driver.
A woman,
standing,
watches a little girl
run through the tall grass.

— Julie Lim (grade 8)

Before students freewrite on the picture of their choice, I begin by reading the following: Larry Leavis's "Edward Hopper, *Hotel,* 1931," as I hold up the reproduction; William Carlos Williams's "Landscape with the Fall of Icarus" and W. H. Auden's "Musée des Beaux Arts," while I show them Brueghel's *Icarus;* and Ferlenghetti's "In Goya's greatest scenes," as I show them Goya's early work and the "dark" work that followed.

Following this pattern, I read student examples while holding up the appropriate reproductions. The students then peruse the different artworks propped about the room, and each student selects one for his or her freewriting. Some of the works I intend to display in the future — exposing students to exceptional visual arts — include the following:

> Rembrandt's *Head of Christ*
> Salvador Dali's *Christ of St. John of the Cross* (the Crucifixion viewed from above)
> Hans Holbein's *Dead Christ* (emphasizing physical death)
> Ansel Adams's photograph *Clearing Winter Storm*
>
> Edward J. Steichen's photograph *Rodin — Le Penseur*
> Dürer's *Oswald Krell* (a maniacal, dangerous face)
> Giotto's *The Kiss* (the look of Christ, the look of Judas, just before Judas kisses Christ)
>
> Goya's *Execution of the Rebels on 3rd May, 1808*
> Picasso's *Guernica*
> Edvard Munch's *The Scream*
>
> Edward Hopper's *Nighthawks* (the streets are flat and barren; and the people, seen through the glass of the all-night coffee shop, appear to be sitting in a spaceship)
> Van Gogh's *Bedroom at Arles*
> Picasso's *Three Musicians*
>
> Alfred Stieglitz's photograph *The Steerage*
> Seurat's *Sunday Afternoon on the Isle of La Grande Jatte*
> M. C. Escher's *Ascending and Descending* (duplicate men infinitely ascending and descending, circularly, impossibly, the same square staircase)
>
> Caravaggio's *The Calling of St. Matthew*
> Botticelli's *St. Augustine* (the inspired scholar)
> Gertrude Kasebier's photograph *Blessed Art Thou among Women* (a girl in the wings about to go on stage)

Examples of students' Visual Response Poems follow.

Bosch's *Detail from Hell*

In Hell there is no rest for the weary,
No time for sleep.
There are constant wars,
Armies amassing for battle
In the fiery planes
Of chaos:
Keys   Chains   Mandolins
. . . and Skulls

Arrows whine as bird creatures smoke from the pipe,

And a blade comes down from above
To split the space between two ears.
Hiding places for the multitudes.

Giant insects converse with men,
Bored-men sink in the quagmire,
Banners wave, and the armies gather.

— David Auerswald (grade 8)

Ansel Adams' *Moonrise*

A pale, white eye in the sky, veined
        with thick, grey patches of mist
Stares from a black, starless, void
        far above the mountains
Onto a row of dull, brown houses.

Tumbleweed litters the dry, desert
        floor like balls of crumpled paper.
Among the dead houses are bone-white
        gravestone crosses standing crookedly in
                their places
Stuck carelessly in the hard ground.
They lean sideways, forwards, and
        backwards
As gaunt as beggars.

Is there life in this place
        besides the moon's searching eye?

A town full of ghosts carries no such
        thing.

— Julie Latham (grade 8)

James Clarke Hook's *Word from the Missing*

The monotonous,
crashing of waves,
sinks into my skull.

My feet heavy,
in the sand,
as I trod along the shore.

The children,
scurry,
searching through the morgue,
of debris,
like scavengers.
As they examine a glass flask,
the sun projects a green glow,
on their morbid faces.

I extend,
my flowing arms,
and place,
a decaying board,
in my reed basket.

Word from the missing.

Slowly,
the waves halt,
the children cease to move.
I become frozen,
eternally suspended,
floating,
out to sea.

We, too, are missed.

— Mindy Starn (grade 8)

9. Extended Metaphor

1. Using Extended Metaphor, write a poem about poetry, the poet, or the poem.

2. First, establish through a simile what the poet, for example, is like. (He may be like a magician.) Then, throughout the remainder of the poem, talk about the poet exclusively in terms of the magician: what he does; how he practices, thinks, feels, and so forth.

Flaming Poetry

Poetry is like flames,
which are swift and elusive
dodging realization.

Sparks, like words on the paper,
leap and dance in the
flickering firelight.

The fiery tongues,
formless and shifting shapes
tease the imagination.

Yet for those who see,
through their mind's eye,
they burn up the page.

— Daniel Rosenthal (grade 8)

After reading a number of examples (see chapter 2 for additional student examples), I ask the students to brainstorm, in three columns, the kinds of things that can be compared to poetry, the poet, and the poem. Then they share their lists, adding to the options they've generated themselves.

The adult poems that I read to them include Ferlinghetti's "Constantly Risking Absurdity," William Carlos Williams's "The Poem," Gary Snyder's "As for Poets," Archibald MacLeish's "Ars Poetica," Marianne Moore's "Poetry," and George Oppen's *"Veritus sequitur. . . ."*

Expect students to break the rules — sometimes ingeniously. Examples of students' Extended Metaphor poems follow.

The Mason

The poet is like a mason
He pours his thoughts onto the paper
Then smoothes out the wrinkles

Then a child walks through the wet cement
Making footprints that will soon harden
Forever imprinting your mind

— Heidi Lowrey (grade 7)

The Poet

She stood
Gazing up at the night
Sky exploding into a sea of
Brilliant reds, yellows, greens
Falling, disappearing into darkness

She ignited
Her magic wand
It sparkled, and hundreds of golden raindrops
Showered the driveway

She decorated the dark space before her
Pushing the light into the darkness
Playing, shaping, controlling it
Her designs
Setting into the darkness at
Enormous speeds.
Like a mason laying a sidewalk
She signed her name

Just as her wand fizzled
The magic left her
But the masterpiece remained
in the afterglow

— Sandra Kim (grade 8)

Poets of the Four Seasons

The Spring poets
catch life
in its bud
with promise of figurative pride.

The Summer poets
write best sellers
of arms that
carry and tug,
and sweat that
rolls over eyebrows.

The Autumn poets
like cherished wine
store their poems
for days
of comfort and repose.

The Winter poets
recognize the end.
Temper it
with the glory of immaculate snow
and the joy of Christmas.

— Kelsey Matsu (grade 8)

The Poet

The poet sits in his
dark den
hoping for luck
like a lion waiting
for a wandering kid
to step into the clearing.
The lion, hungrily roars
in anger
and steps out
into the night.
He sees the
blue-starred antelope
attacks
but misses.
In frustration he
kills a groundhog
but to no avail
and walks back
into the darkness
even more unsatisfied.

— unknown student (grade 8)

10. Memory Poem

1. Write a poem based on a memory.

2. It may help you if you speak, in your poem, to the person with whom you shared the experience.

In Memory

When I think of you,
I see you in overalls
burning trash with me in Aiea.
Playing games with me,

telling me to hide from McGarret of "5-0"
I don't see a dying man
in a hospital bed.
I see the comedian who drove my grandmother nuts.
Who played games with me
and picked tangerines off the old tree.

But that was years ago.
And when Grandma died you died too.
Sort of.
When we visited you
you weren't there, were you?
You heard us but the magic was gone.
The fire died
and the tree blew down.

Today's the funeral, Grandpa . . .
Yours.
But they will never bury my memory
of you.

— Gregory Char (grade 8)

As I said earlier, there are some assignments that require only reading
lots of student examples. The Memory Poem assignment is one of
these. If students have been writing any poetry at all, this assignment
guarantees success. No other assignment will put them in touch with
their feelings as well. To their delight, it helps them recall and re-
create the past, as they relive it in the present, crystallizing and
preserving it.

Together with student examples I read aloud D. H. Lawrence's
"Piano," James Wright's "Youth," Rilke's "From a Childhood," Norman
Hindley's "Wood Butcher," and Eric Chock's "Papio."

Then, closing their eyes, students play back the "film" of their
memory before their mind's eye, from the earliest to the most recent
memories, stopping the film whenever they see something interesting,
noting it, and then starting and stopping the film again — creating a
list of memories from which to choose.

Examples of students' Memory Poems follow.

My Mid-day Book

Lying on my bed
Kicking my legs to the rhythm of the story

I must have heard it countless times
I memorized every picture.
I could recite the words forward and backward

But still after having tomato soup with
a toasted cheese sandwich for lunch
I could be found, before my nap, on my
parents' bed.
Waiting . . .
To hear those tricky lines of
Hop on Pop

The words,
Music to my ears.
The pictures,
Always entertaining
Time after time after time.

— Chris Nespeca (grade 8)

Memory Mouse

I still remember your small white teeth
I still have the scars
I still dream about that white fur
I wonder if I should have skinned you
Your fur would make a nice wall hanging
Your claws that were so agile, once clicking and running
about my room. I wish I could still hang you
by the tail, your whiskers twitching in pain
If only you were still here, so I could poke
you with chopsticks, through the bars of your
cage.

— Austin Sloat (grade 7)

My First Boyfriend

My first boyfriend,
It doesn't seem
Possible that I was
Only four.
So young,
But I guess it was
About right.

Nine years ago
I met him;
We were in pre-school
At St. Michael's School,
He had dark brown hair,
Brown eyes, and a fair complexion.
His expression was always
One of
Mischief, I remember.

I was perhaps an inch taller with
Green eyes and
Light hair in a pixie cut,
I resembled a chubby elf.

We used to run and play
Together, tag and see-saw.
We went trick-or-treating
With each other that year;
He was an adorable
Scoobie-Doo,
And me an angel,
Hard to believe.

While our mothers talked
We used to jump on his bed
Until we broke it.
But oh, how much fun it was
Bouncing to touch the sky,
Or at least,
The ceiling.

— Julie Latham (grade 8)

Memories

At age four my major milestone
        was standing on my head.
Weeks of practice were spent
        accomplishing this feat.
Shaky starts became more confident
        until I could stand
Unaided at will.
When the grandparents came
        for their annual visit

I planned to be the star of the show
    Dazzling them with my feats of balance.
Slowly walking to center stage
    I stood on my head.
Grandfather slowly bent down,
    and joined me on his head.
(He also did cartwheels.)

         — Malia Hale (grade 8)

Big Sis

My sister,
now 18,
has left for college.
I can still see her chubby face smiling,
as she left for San Fransisco,
going to Santa Clara.
The last time I saw her was when she walked down a corridor,
entering a United Airlines airplane,
the scent of her carnation and tuberose lei,
spreading throughout the terminal.
I can still remember her when she was 12,
her teeth bearing braces,
on her awkward face,
her big round nose,
smack in the center of her pimples.
Now her face has caught up with her nose,
she, of course, has no braces,
her pimples aren't as bad,
and her thighs are now thick with cellulite.
But I'll miss her,
mostly because I have no one to talk to,
except my older brother,
but him, why would I want to talk to him?
He usually grunts.

         — Shannon Bremner (grade 7)

11. Bitterness Poem

1. Write a poem that illustrates the feeling of bitterness, anger, protest, or even hate.

2. Despite the negative feeling, the one requirement is that the poem, as always, be honestly expressed.

Rage

Dealing with my mother's cancer
gives me enough anger
to last forever
why my mother?!
What'd she do to deserve this?!
sometimes coming home
finding my mom sick in bed
with pains in her chest
that keep her from speaking
gets my depression and hate
tangled within each other
what am I supposed to say or do?
the fault I have
that gathers inside me
when I've gotten angry and yelled
        at her
it's hard for me to talk to her
with all my hatred
toward the disease I detest
I am so frightened
that one day
it could cause my mother's . . .
        DEATH.

                    — Tara Osborne (grade 8)

About two months later, in December, this student's mother died, but
during the interval Tara read to her mother all the poetry she had
written for class and for herself, even though the mother, toward the
end, could not hear the words. But as Tara had written later, she knew
her mother had felt her voice, her love . . . her prayer. Afterwards,
Tara duplicated her poetry and subsequent work and sent them to
others whose loved ones were dying. Because she too had experienced
their struggle, their grief, their anger and depression, she felt that
hearing from someone similarly tried would provide understanding
and comfort and would encourage in them her strength. In such ways,
poetry heals.

Students vent powerful feelings, disciplined through art — which
licenses their public expression and encourages the heart to speak its
truth, however bitter it may be. In this assignment, often more than
in any other, the young writers seem to speak primarily to themselves.

Among the works of adult poetry I read aloud to students are Langston Hughes's "Theme from English B," Calvin C. Hernton's "The Distant Drum," Theodore Roethke's "Dolor," an Eskimo poem called "Hunger," and Matthew Arnold's "Dover Beach."

Examples of students' Bitterness Poems follow.

Divorce

I sit remembering that day
in the courtroom
the day when
my mother
and father
said they didn't love each other
anymore

But what if
they never did love
each other and married because
of me?
Couldn't be
for the time wasn't right

But could it be
me, who made them
stop loving,
caring,
sharing?
That could be a
possibility

What would happen
if they stopped loving
me?
Can parents divorce
their children?
What if they never did
love me?

Thoughts of childhood
seem silly now
But the feelings . . .

Stay

— Marion Stockert (grade 8)

Bitterness

I distinctly remember when I
Was six
When my mom and dad told me
I was only legally theirs

My "real" mom
Only eighteen at the time

Couldn't undertake a baby
Feed it
Clothe it
Educate it

Maybe even love it
Just a little

How could she
When she was still in school
Still
Learning
Growing
Deciphering life
And unconsciously crying out for a little
Love herself?

I know her name.
I know who she is

Now she's married and living a happy
Life

At thirty-two

Childless

But maybe in a way she's paying
(Like I always have)

For being too greedy
It's kind of sad

Maybe I'll forgive her
Maybe I won't

Because

On that cold dark day
When she gave me away

She pretty much changed.
My life

— Malia Hickok (grade 8)

My Nana, Rita

Lunch with
my least favorite grandmother,
Rita.

She looks glamorous
high heels, well dressed, red lipstick
straight from Beverley Hills
she's actually cheap,
comes from her tradition

She wanted pizza for lunch
that day,

but this place was too expensive
and that place was filthy
she needs cheap cleanliness

finally she decided on a Pizzeria
a cheap one
where we ate
thin, saucy pizza with only cheese
exactly the kind I hate

She is a cheap phony,
Rita is,
thin and saucy, like the pizza.

— Pam Friedlander (grade 8)

Teased

I can't stand teasing.
It twists me like licorice
until I
break.
Tears swell in my eyes
and a fist clenches my throat, pinching it.
Embarrassment rolls down my cheek.

I try to wipe it away before anyone notices.
Too late
they see my eyes, blushing.
Now they think I'm
a crybaby
Hiccup,
they think it's all in fun
I know it's supposed to be,
why can't they stop!
C'mon, get a hold of yourself.
You're such a crybaby —
see what scars mosquitos leave.

— Keli Sato (grade 7)

Daughter

Why must you think you're the best?
I am queen of this family, and don't you forget it
I worry about you at those night clubs, partying, having fun
I wish I could be with you.
You challenge me to a sport I was once good at.
You think you're so pretty.
You tell me I lived in the Ice Age
That I am
Old
and
Dumb
Wait until you're my age and you look back at yourself.
You'll wish you were young and pretty.
There I will be at the other side of the mirror . . .

— Malia Rego (grade 7)

12. Paradox Poem

Write a poem illustrating a paradox. A paradox is a seemingly self-contradictory statement that expresses a possible truth — pointing ultimately to mystery.

Brother-Sister

Like two scorpions in a jar
Waiting for the other to turn its back
So the attack can begin

Like referees
Watching each move the other makes
Then blowing a whistle on the defender
For the parents

Yet, they are an actor and an actress
For when one is in pain
The other feels the grief too

— Tina Hines (grade 7)

After reading Whitman's "The Compost" (where life is born from dregs, refuse, and the remains of the dead), Robinson Jeffers's "The Great Explosion" (where "faceless violence, [is] the root of all things"), and student examples, I read "Everything and Nothing" from Borges's *Labyrinths*. In short, this parable recounts the history of Shakespeare's role-playing: as an actor, director, playwright, and businessman — the creator of characters *par excellence*. According to Borges (1964, 248–49), at the time of death, Shakespeare, finding himself in the presence of God, asks God, "I who have been so many men in vain want to be one and myself." For Borges, self-identity apart from others is impossible, for

> The voice of the Lord answered from a whirlwind: "Neither am I anyone; I have dreamt the world as you dreamt your work, my Shakespeare, and among the forms in my dream are you, who like myself are many and no one."

Examples of students' Paradox Poems follow.

Mother Says

Mother says
"Say hello"
"Be polite"
"Be nice"
"Be friendly"
"Say thank you"
"Speak when you are spoken to"
"Say bye-bye"

A child grows up
Believing
Grown-ups are
Honest
Loving
Caring

Mother says
"Don't talk to strangers"
"Don't be polite"
"Don't be friendly"
"Don't do as you are told"
"Don't speak when you are spoken to"
"Say bye-bye"

"And run!"

— Gregg Loo (grade 8)

Second Sight

I
Do not know
What it is
To not see

The sunrise
A flower blooms
On the horizon

It happens every day
It is no privilege of mine
To see this birth

My brother, fellow human
Does not see
The sights of life

He does not see

But feels what
I cannot feel
Hears the voice
Of wind

He does not
See this land
But sees far beyond
To what this land
Will become

Sensing through closed
Wide eyes
What I could never
Take in
Through my blind eyes.

— Laura Murray (grade 7)

Elements

Fire —
     warmth, comfort;
     yet scorching,
     like rage;
          destructive.

Wind —
     cool and free;
          a dancer;
     but sharp and cutting;
          dirty blood,
               from a knife.
     Harsh words.

Water —
     flowing forever,
          like time;
     eroding land, life.

Land —
     provides food,
     a home,
          sustains mankind.
     A burial place.

Fire expands air.
Wind makes fire grow.
Water encourages life.
Land absorbs water.

But, fire, wind
     burn.
Water pulls
     out to sea.
And land will again
     explode
          into
                    fire
                    wind
                    water.

                         — Ashley Maynard (grade 8)

Death

Death makes room for new ideas,
In nature it helps the living,
It takes one on to a new world,
A one-way journey to never-ever land.
It relieves pain,
A necessary part of life.

It hurts.

— Edward Henigin (grade 8)

13. Awe Poem

Write a poem, reliving the experience of awe.

Michael Jordan

Running with speed beyond speed
Muscles tightening, rippling
A child of heaven, jumping immeasurable heights
Leaping amazing distances
Gracefully gliding over the others
As if walking on air
High-fiving the hand of God
Touching the clouds and swooping
Down
Slam dunk!
Touching the alien ground like a
Feather

— Alec Rice (grade 7)

Let me repeat, in short, the strategy I explained more effusively in chapter 2 under Presenting Assignments (page 21).

1. Optional: lead students through Keats's "On First Looking into Chapman's Homer."
2. Tell them a personal experience of awe.
3. Read aloud works that arouse awe, such as the following:

    W. S. Merwin's "Leviathan" (awesome size, power)

    Ishmael's talk of the sperm whale's head from *Moby Dick* (awesome mystery)

    Macbeth's "tomorrow" speech (awesome language, attitude)

The opening of Milton's *Paradise Lost* (awesome promise)

God's response to Job (awesome presence)

4. Read aloud student examples.
5. Students brainstorm experiences of awe and then freewrite a half page on three of these instances.
6. Students freewrite a definition for awe and share their definitions with the class.
7. Students write an Awe Poem based on one of their freewritings.

Examples of students' Awe Poems follow.

Ruler of One

Reeling in the bait.

Depressed

Not one bite.

Slowly

neeeeeee

like the sound of
thunder

the fish makes a run

snap
free.

for that moment

ruler of something.

Exuberant.

rejunvenated

hope.

— Ricky Kakazu (grade 7)

Marvelous Show

Even Pele celebrated '85.
The early January evening
glowed like a sparkler.

Driving to the eruption
the ribboning road
seemed endless.
The dark forms of trees
played hide and seek with the volcano.

Finally, the fountaining licks
of lava
burst into view.

The massive column towered over me,
casting crimson shadows
into the black night.

Only the stars
winking back in acknowledgement.

— Corey Matsuoka (grade 8)

Bird

The packed auditorium
Alive
As her sturdy body raced
Like a horse set free from a stall
A gazelle — full speed

A cannon fires
Her body flew
Tucking twirling
A football violently whizzing through the air
To crack the earth
With its force

Gymnastics used to be just
Another sport
Until I saw Mary Lou

Feeling like
I was caught in
A whirlwind
Pushed into
Another dimension

My heart soaring
Like a comet
Like Franklin with
His kite
Electricity surging through
My brain

Proud of my country
Proud of this
Magic girl
For she could become
Something humans weren't
Meant to be

A bird

Golden feathers
Glistening from a ribbon
Hanging from her neck

— Laura Murray (grade 7)

14. Teacher Poem

Write a poem describing a teacher whom you find, for one reason or another, unforgettable. Try to see that teacher as clearly and honestly as you can.

Drill

A retired,
Navy Captain,
that should have.

He would pace
through the format
of desks,
his dull, grey,
wooden-soled shoes
resounding
through the Pinesol-clean room,
like soldiers' rifles
clattering against their metallic
chests.
His parasite-like presence,
looming,
over you.
A steel voice clutching your brain.

Even when he left the room,
no one dare stir,
for his footsteps were no longer
harsh.
They became those
of a moccasined Indian,
Stalking his prey.
Pray?
That you must.

— Mindy Starn (grade 8)

Tell stories. Students love stories, especially about us. I begin by telling
my students stories about three teachers whom I can't forget. The first,
about Professor Lardas, I recounted at the end of chapter 1, and the
second, about Professor Kriegel, at the end of chapter 2. The third
story is about a teacher (I can't recall her name) who, I think, was
blonde and young and who taught us second or third grade. Those
years remain hazy for me. The classroom that day was very bright; it
must have been in June with the sun shining through the tall windows
along the length of the room. Everything glowed and was full of light.
All of us, I remember, were reading in our seats, though I'm sure we
were chatting. One by one we were called to read to our teacher in
private. I might have been nervous, since at that time I was reading
very poorly. And I guess I read poorly that day. So poorly, in fact,
that to the shock of my classmates, the teacher lifted the reader above
her shoulder and flung it in disgust to the floor. It bounced end over
end and skidded to a stop at the base of a student's desk, opened and
face down. For what seemed a long time no one moved or seemed to
breathe. But, from what I recall, I was the least affected by the teacher's
outburst. What I remember best is the stunned and frightened look in
my classmates' faces. What was wrong? Why? Nothing could ever be
that bad. I felt for them. This happened so long ago that today I am
not sure that any of this ever happened.

Examples of students' Teacher Poems follow.

And He Teaches at Punahou?

Playing "She's so Unusual"
after school.
Hanging Cyndi Lauper posters
around the room
with her blazing red hair and make-up
it looks like Picasso was her beautician.
Asking what happened over the weekend,
telling us about teaching in Amsterdam,
bringing Vegemite to school for tasting,
dressing as Reptile Man for Halloween,
going sky-diving,
taking pictures of blue starfish in Fiji.
Explaining why he puts Oil of Olay
on his sun-puffed eyes,
thinking of names for our mathematical battle teams,
boys against girls.
Betting us that Philadelphia would beat the Orioles,
writing a poem in chalk
while we did our Friday math quiz.

Sitting behind his front desk
with windmill, calendar of rare words,
answer book, and signed picture of Miss Chinatown.
Wearing Magnum-style shirts on his thin body
and a mustache that never quite
matched his curly brown hair.
His voice had a resonance jello,
it wasn't built for yelling.
We learned more than math or
science,
we learned how to howl at the moon!

— Keli Sato (grade 7)

The Soul of a Teacher

The teacher smiles
as she hands back
the homework.

Her smile isn't
a cruel, mocking
smile of victory
over her students.
It's a cheery
sunny smile.

I glance at my paper.

The lipstick red
D smiles viciously at me,
enjoying my defeat,
insulting my intelligence,
hiding behind
a mask of innocence.

— Frank Shotwell (grade 8)

Teacher

Bearer
of the fruits
of knowledge.
Body compressed
as the knowledge
in his mind.

Out of his mind
and mouth
come beauty.
From our hands
and mind
onto paper
from pen,
the ink
paints
a picture
of his mind's
eye,
through
our own.

Mildly
he teaches
that though
certain words
may glitter
are not gold
and have no place
among ideas
that are gems.

Be oneself,
use intuition
and guts,
his doctrine.
His magic
teachings
transform
our words
on paper
to mirrors
of our souls.

— Reid Oshiro (grade 8)

Mr. Holbrook

Mr. Holbrook, why do you make jokes about how people look?
Do you think it's funny to match people up? I think it is.
The way you talk and laugh in a jolly ole way.
It makes me laugh and makes Katie laugh like a seal.

Your favorite enemy, Mr. Brown, the way you talk about him
    makes me laugh and practically fall off my seat.
Sometimes I wish I were you, because you can make a person
    smile like sunshine and laugh like a hyena.
Sometimes I am glad I am myself because I can
    soak up all your joy and happiness.

— Julie Kometani (grade 7)

15. Form Poem

1. Write a poem using, for your own purposes, a commonplace reference form.

2. Consider all the conventional verbal forms printed on things throughout your house. In what way could you use any one of them in fulfilling your intentions?

Dictionary

Watch —
counter of time

Watches —
something an over-protective mother does

Watched —
a sinking feeling of eyes

— Jessica Slater (grade 7)

Students brainstorm together. I encourage them to consult the following: dictionary, thesaurus (for slang alternatives, in Hindi); encyclopedia, grammar books, *Who's Who* (Who's Not, Who Shouldn't Be); indexes, statistical reports, bibliographies (for suicides, bag ladies); timetables (Flight 6: for South Bend, Styx, or Simony); prefaces, tables of contents, conversion tables and rates of exchange (2 pints blood = 1 kiss); programs, menus (appropriate to funerals, Halloween, mothers-in-law); recipes, instructions (for SATs, making poisons, using chopsticks); vitae, records and transcripts (for prisoners, pets); résumés (for Charles Manson, Michelangelo, your uncle); case studies, dedications, epitaphs (Keats: "Here lies one whose name was writ on water"); syllabi (for entomology, vengeance, dating); telephone books, lobby directories, health records (for principals, junk-food addicts); five-year plans, travel itinerary (to Brooklyn and beyond); commandments, bylaws, codes (of conduct, jealousy, ants); allegiances, promises, oaths, contracts, subpoenas (for Christ, Don Rickles, Idi Amin); certificates (birth, identity, sanity); calendars, registration forms, TV guides, horoscopes, organizational charts (à la Dante's circle of Hell); road signs, content labels (May be hazardous to adults); rankings (of angels, feet, phobias); labels on museum pieces, prescriptions (by dentists, for pimples); directions (as on the lobby directory in the philosophy building: Why are you here?); diagnoses, prognoses, classified ads (For Sale: X-rays of famous noses); trivia questions (Who invented AIDS?); maps, geographical distances (from Reprieve, North Dakota); book reports, tardy slips, resolutions, obituaries, last wills and testaments.

The more we encourage the students to play, the merrier, louder, and more imaginative they will be. Instigated by the teacher, the class's "crazy" emphases become the students' emphases as they work on their poems.

Examples of students' Form Poems follow.

Nutrition Information on a Teenager's Life

Homework	2%
Sleep	2%
Beach	6%
Getting Yelled At	10%
Shopping	20%
In Front of Mirror	30%
School	30%

— Chelsea Wade (grade 8)

Career Man

I
The general
Stood before my troops
And saluted inward.

A bookshelf
15 inches wide
Glows
And stretches
Over the whole desk
Rendering other things invisible
Superimposing itself.

AsimovBenfordBrunnerBusbyFarmer
    HarrisonKnightLaumerNiven
    WellsVillarWambaughVanVogt.

Once again:
1. Asimov, Isaac
2. Benford, Gregory
3. Brunner, John
4. Busby, F.M.
5. Farmer, Philip
6. Harrison, Harry
7. Knight, Damon
8. Laumer, Keith
9. Niven, Lawrence
10. Wells, Herman
11. Villar, Joseph
12. Wambaugh, Joseph
13. Van Vogt, A.E.

All present.

Good Night.

— Sam Onaga (grade 8)

Thesaurus: *Alien*

rain —
shower, precipitation, rainstorm,
downpour, drizzle, bestow, lavish,
shower upon.

alone —
apart, solitary, individual

My cheek presses against the cool
window pane.
Gray storm surrounds me.
Cut off from the world.

— Mindy Starn (grade 8)

American

Ingredients:
German, Italian, Dutch, Mexican, Spanish,
Russian, Chinese, Indian, Polish, Irish, Asian,
African, French, etc.

Warning

Americans may seem kind and generous at first, but
may turn on you and become vicious. They may be
armed and try to hurt you. Exercise extreme
caution when handling.

— James Byrer (grade 7)

16. Self Portrait

1. *Write a poem, nine to eleven stanzas in length, about yourself.*
2. *Options:*

   See yourself from various angles, in various settings, at different times, seasons, ages; involved in various actions, captured in various moods.

   Describe yourself using a variety of voices: your mother's, your brother's, your friend's, your teacher's, a stranger's.

   In addition to using I, *you can also refer to yourself as* he *or* she, *as many fiction writers do.*

   In addition to making statements, you can ask questions, issue orders, moan, and shout, speaking to whomever you wish.

3. *Remember that what you are after is character, personality: what the artist tries to capture in painting a portrait.*

> The Strange Kid with the Red Face
>
> . . . Between shelves
> Then he stumbles between the doors
> Of the BLC
> And smirks.
>
> Outside there's a noisey clamor
> But inside
> Is one
> Reading.
>
> His room
> Is full of
> > Books
> > Rubbish
> > Insects (dead)
> In shambles.
> So
> On the bed
> Is he.
>
> The cockroach
> Turned over
> Waved its legs.
> STOMP
> He picks it up
> Sails it
> To his sister
> Who screams.

His father:
He always
Creeps up
While I'm watching television
And
SCREAMS
Giving me a heart attack
Stupid *ss.

His mother:
He hides
So I can't talk to him
About his dirty room
    the dirty kitchen
      the dog's mistakes
      the leaf-filled patio
Oh, there he is —
SAMMY!

His sister:
He trips
    and scares
    and pushes into dog excrement
    and antagonizes

Me
He thinks
He is smart
Because he reads unintelligible books
F*C**NG *SSH*L* *ITCH

Peewee:
He reads
Science ficition
And trades books
But
    He makes
      short
      practical
      personal
        jokes
Damn Spam.

The librarian:
That strange kid
With the red face
Dumps

And stacks neatly
The books
On the desk and says:
"Please"
In a dead
    Phlegmatic
    Broken-down
    Rasp
He drags out of sight
Crumpled
Sad
Taking the Dr. Seusses and Vonneguts.

And so he lives on,
Petty little human,
Antagonizing
Thinking
Reading
Talking
Fleeing
And
Laughing from a distance.

                — Sam Onaga (grade 8)

I lead the class through Wallace Stevens's "Thirteen Ways of Looking at a Blackbird," showing them the various ways the poet sees and speaks. Next we read students' Self Portrait poems, adding options to the repertoire begun by Stevens.

Then I recommend to students that in their own poems they speak in the third person, distancing, as far as possible, all that they have been, all that they are, and all that they can be from the artist, whose immediate purpose is to see accurately. Though the use of the third person does not eliminate sentimentality or undue harshness (they can be very hard on themselves), it does facilitate their doing themselves greater justice — balancing better the moral, spiritual, and psychological visions they have of themselves.

Despite the various points of view or screens we may use, speaking about oneself "honestly" is titanically difficult at any age. But rather than a test of character, confidence, and conviction, the Self Portrait assignment (speaking about oneself) accommodates a healthful reconception and acceptance of oneself. In short, the students grow more comfortable with themselves, knowing the moment, which contains all the past, is transitory, and the next is infinite potential.

Examples of students' Self Portrait poems follow.

Self Portrait

** 1 **

Too tall, a giraffe,
Thin white legs
Protruding from a
Sadly underdeveloped
Torso.
An American Ethiopian.

** 2 **

My generally, friendly,
Cuddly, studly, dudley
Disposition
Impresses
(Sometimes)
(If I'm lucky.)
As Prince says,
"Baby, I ain't got no money
But, honey, I'm rich on personality
Yep, that's me."

** 3 **

"Ha ha ha! Batman! Wimp!"
Very funny.
An PHPTFPH to you, too!

** 4 **

I could be handsome
If only
        My face
        My hair
        My legs
        My clothes . . .
Too bad.

** 5 **

Q: Heavy Metal?
Yes, absolutely!
I love it
Q: What else?
Anything that sounds good.

** 6 **

"BMX Freestyle!"
Music to my ears.
My bike's shot,
But it works to
Hold the
Kuapa Kai
Backhop record: 150

** 7 **

Soy cansado!
Sleep,   sleep,   sleep.
I'm tired.

** 8 **

I don't like
              Broccoli
              Bananas
              Brussel sprouts
              Squash
              Sweet potatoes
              Zucchini,
All vegetables.
Only candy is good.

** 9 **

"Psst! Who do you like?"
Think I'm gonna tell you?

** 10 **

I have fun,
At least I like to.
If it weren't for
              Homework
              Jerks
              Donkey pores
I love life,
I wouldn't give it up for
Anything.

— Edward Henigin (grade 8)

Self Portrait

I wonder,
as I look into
the mirror,
what it would be like
to be outside me,
and look at myself
inside.

I am a kaleidoscope,
bits and pieces
changing,
never the same.

As I walk along the shore,
sand crunches beneath my feet.
The waves
rise and fall, rise and fall,
and always shall
no matter what I do.

I am petty
cast away by wind and sea.
I tell myself
it is not your fault
do not let it bother you
for if you do it will be.

Waves halt,
the sun and moon are suspended,
the wind's only torment, silence,
I do not notice.

I go through
all the motions of life
forgetting words.

Wandering
through meadows and creeks
sensing something
at every turn.
Finding nothing.

I hide
in the cozy warmth of rain.
Storm surrounds me;
I surround it.
me, still.
Telling me my life
will be
a monotonous rise and fall.

The wind whispers,
"Nothing's fair."
And dries
my tears.

                              — Mindy Starn (grade 8)

17. Invitation Poem

*1. Write a poem that invites readers to join you on a tour through your
poetry book.*

*2. As a preview of your trip, provide glimpses of the strange, grotesque,
and beautiful things you've written about, which they will soon encounter.*

                    Invitation!

As I ride in awe
On the Music Fest,
I think
About the crunchy, crispy, delicious salad
I had,
And how, just awhile ago
I smelled
Dirty, stinky, P.E. clothes
Oh well —
That's the past
Oh no, we're going faster!
Whoa!
Stop!
The ride's over.
Oh no!
My invitation
To the Halloween party!
I must get home and R.S.V.P.!

When I arrived
At my house,
I climbed our stairs,
I thought
About when I was little,
Running on tiptoes
To my kindergarten teacher
Who was so nice to me.
I turn on the TV
And ick!
Monday Night Football!
My hound dog starts to bark
From the back porch.
It is finally the end
Of the day,
But not of adventure.

Come with me.

— Jennifer Hall (grade 8)

The Invitation Poem is the second to last poem that students will write for the quarter, and serves as the opening poem of their poetry books. Having written over twenty-five poems, they have much material from which to draw upon to whet the reader's appetite.

More important, in looking back on what they have written, students come to see that a poetry book is what they have been working toward all along. And, suddenly, their books will soon be real. Now they begin to believe; they can almost see the books, bound, in their own hands.

Examples of students' Invitation Poems follow.

Invitation

Come with me into a world
Where a child turns into a sorcerer,
As quickly as a drop of rain
Falls from a gray sea
To a plush, green meadow
Moving with the wind,
Each blade tilting,
To the same direction,
At different heights,
At different moments,

So much like people
In this world;
Where before a mirror
Stands that child
Reflecting the sheep,
Near a pack of wolves,
Under that dark, cloudy sky.

— Sheree Kon (grade 8)

Invitation

Come and take a look with me,
All of which I wrote for thee,
The sorrow and the anger burning
Just an amateur poet learning.
Come and see the joy tomorrow
From another life I borrow,
See the envy, see the greed,
Growing, fruitful, from a seed.
Concrete, what is that?
Nothing like the words I spat,
Yet I followed what he preached, what he told,
Eventually learning to shape and mold,
Seeing nothing like before,
Viewing thoughts I store, explore.
Remembering bitter moments with tears,
Tears, shedding my mind of fears.
So come, be part of my world,
Capture ideas, my mind, my curls.

— Kim Wong (grade 8)

Invitation

I sing of C's; of Coke, comforts, coping, and church.
With these, I give to thee
The almighty book that will forever be.
I write of D's; of dogs, and ducks,
Hoping that with these poems you will be struck.
I write of F's; of feelings and fleas,
Commanding you not to laugh at these, please.
I sing of M's; of myself, of miner, and mother.
I ask you to read these before any other.
I write of an N; of a so-called nothing,

With a miracle turned out to be something.
I write of an R; of a relational.
I hope you will find it to be sensational.
I sing of S's; of the sky, of songs, of streams, of
     the sun, of sunsets, and sunrises.
I'm informing you so there won't be any surprises.
I laugh of a T; a teacher,
Those that tend to turn into preachers.
I write of W's; of water and walking,
I wish you would please stop talking.
So I may present to you this book,
That I hope you — Oh, here, take a look.

                    — Stephen Di Mauro (grade 8)

Invitation

I sing of silver grass and loneliness,
of earth and loam and deserts
filled with roses.

I write of earthworms, plow's wakes,
and dusty roads leading nowhere,
and of the moon and myself;
I wander seeking light
knowing I will find it someday.

                    — Mindy Starn (grade 8)

18. End Poem

Write an End Poem, perhaps about "ends," ending your poetry book.

The End of Time

A flower opens its petals as wide as it can
As a ballpoint pen drops its last inch of ink
An old man falls asleep for the last time
A clock tick tocks its last minute
A light drizzle falls from the sky
     right after a heavy rainstorm
The songs become faint, can't be heard from a distance
As last autumn leaves fall from the trees
The carolers stop singing
The children take their Halloween costumes off
The Easter baskets are given out

A child's hope is lost as he fails to complete his job
The sun sets as the sky gets darker
As a relationship ends because a person displays hate
An artist's last stroke
A child's faith is lost as someone defies him
The last snowflake as the winter melts
A candle spurts its last flicker of light
As a writer dots the last period of his poem.

— Misa Okada (grade 8)

I ask students to consider what kind of poem would be a fitting or appropriate end for their poetry books. What is the final message for the reader? The following End Poems were written by students after each had considered his or her poetry as a whole.

Afternoon

Down the land,
The crystal water flows,
Etching its pathway in the
Rock.

A fish jumps,
A flup.
Its scales shine
In the sunlight
Blinding me a
Moment.

The sun high,
Warming by body,
Feeding the plants that
Surround me.

I throw a rock,
Ripples on the water
Wrinkling my reflection
Fifty years.

Soon, I leave
Taking one last look,
I see the sunset
Painted on the water
With my eyes
Staring back at me.

— Vanessa Kawamura (grade 8)

The End

The lights on my window sill
Reflect the moon
Like oceans of glass

By standing on my bed
and peering out through the windows
I can just barely see
The edge of a
Golden sun setting
And the pinks and oranges
That surround it

I thought of all the things that
Happened that day and
Laughed
Cried
Got mad
Wondered
Worried
Smiled

The porch light outside is on
And a tiny swarm of termites
Dance around it

The crickets are coming out
Singing of life
A concert

I bid the sun good-bye
As it slips over the earth
And get ready for the next time

It opens up.

— Sandra Kim (grade 8)

The End

And so ends the story,
Not much of a story
But
Two
Torturous months
In English.

The poems,
All through
           Sweat
           Blood
           Tears
Came to you,
Just for you.

This time has helped
To show
If I try,
I can succeed
(With flying colors,
Of course).

Poems have been
Beaten into my
Mind.
I have started
              Eating
              Sleeping
              Thinking
Living my life,
As a poem.

And it is
Now
Being brutally
Yanked from
Under my feet.

— Edward Henigin (grade 8)

Works Cited

Berthoff, Ann E. 1981. *The Making of Meaning: Metaphors, Models, and Maxims for Writing Teachers.* Upper Montclair, N.J.: Boynton/Cook.

Borges, Jorge Luis. 1964. "Everything and Nothing." In *Labyrinths: Selected Short Stories and Other Writings,* edited by Donald A. Yates and James E. Irby. New York: New Directions Books.

Crane, Hart. 1966. *The Complete Poems and Selected Letters of Hart Crane.* New York: Anchor Books.

Elbow, Peter. 1981. *Writing with Power: Techniques for Mastering the Writing Process.* New York: Oxford University Press.

Eliot, T. S. 1950. "Tradition and the Individual Talent." In *Selected Essays,* rev. ed. New York: Harcourt, Brace and World.

Koch, Kenneth. 1974. *Rose, Where Did You Get That Red? Teaching Great Poetry to Children.* New York: Random House.

————. 1980. *Wishes, Lies, and Dreams: Teaching Children to Write Poetry.* New York: Harper and Row.

Lorca, Federico Garcia. 1955. "The Duende: Theory and Divertissment." In *Poet in New York.* New York: Grove Press.

May, Rollo. 1975. *The Courage to Create.* New York: Norton.

Pound, Ezra. 1960. *ABC of Reading.* New York: New Directions Books.

Rilke, Rainer Maria. 1965. "The Penetration of Things." In *The Modern Tradition: Backgrounds of Modern Literature,* edited by Richard Ellmann and Charles Feidelson, Jr. New York: Oxford University Press.

Tsujimoto, Joseph I. 1984. "Re-Visioning the Whole." *English Journal* 73, no. 5 (September): 52–55.

Author

Joseph I. Tsujimoto currently teaches middle school students at Punahou School in Honolulu, Hawaii. He is a teacher/consultant with the Hawaii Writing Project, serves on the Advisory Board of the National Writing Project, and is a member of the English Coalition Conference. He has published fiction, poetry, and essays in various journals.